Table of Contents (MOS – Wo

- [CONTENT UPDATES](#) ... 3
- [ABOUT THIS BOOK](#) ... 3
- [PREPARING YOUR TRIAL INSTALLATION](#) ... 7
- [THE PRIMARY WORD INTERFACE](#) ... 9
- [WORD DOCUMENTS](#) ... 12
- [WORD DOCUMENT FORMATTING AND PAGE LAYOUT](#) ... 25
- [TEXT FORMATTING AND LISTS IN WORD](#) ... 34
- [PARAGRAPHS AND SECTIONS IN WORD](#) ... 41
- [TABLES IN WORD](#) ... 47
- [REFERENCES IN WORD](#) ... 50
- [BIBLIOGRAPHY, ENDNOTES, FOOTNOTES AND CAPTIONS IN WORD](#) ... 56
- [BUILDING BLOCKS, QUICK PARTS, SHAPES, PICTURES AND OTHERS](#) ... 61
- [MACRO AND SHORTCUT KEYS IN WORD](#) ... 68
- [THE PRIMARY EXCEL INTERFACE](#) ... 72
- [WORKSHEETS AND WORKBOOKS](#) ... 75
- [COPYING, PASTING AND FILLING CELLS AND RANGES](#) ... 88
- [FORMATTING CELLS AND RANGES](#) ... 97
- [LISTS, TABLES AND CHARTS IN EXCEL](#) ... 103

FORMULAS AND FUNCTIONS **110**

TEXTBOXES AND OTHER OBJECTS IN EXCEL **115**

MACRO AND SHORTCUT KEYS IN EXCEL **121**

THE OUTLOOK ENVIRONMENT AND SETTINGS **123**

OUTLOOK EMAIL FORMATTING **142**

MORE ON OUTLOOK EMAIL MESSAGING **151**

OUTLOOK SCHEDULING **160**

TASKS AND NOTES **172**

CONTACTS AND CONTACT GROUPS **176**

CONTENT UPDATES

ExamREVIEW is an independent content developer not associated/affiliated with Microsoft. The exams described are the trademarks/properties of Microsoft. We at ExamREVIEW develop study material entirely on our own. Our material is fully copyrighted. Braindump is strictly prohibited. We provide essential knowledge contents, NOT any generalized "study system" kind of "pick-the-right-answer-every time" techniques or "visit this link" referrals.

MS Office, Word, Excel, PowerPoint, Outlook, MOS…etc are the trademarks of Microsoft Corp. We are not affiliated with or endorsed by Microsoft Corp.

All orders come with LIFE TIME FREE UPDATES. When you find a newer version of the purchased product all you need to do is to go and download. **Please check our web site regularly.**

http://www.examreview.net/free_updates.htm

About this book

With the MOS 2013 exams, you will be presented with a project to build. Therefore, real world experience with the software is highly important. You should start by learning how to perform individual tasks. Then you need to "chain up" your skills and apply them on the project to produce a meaningful outcome as required by the exam questions.

The Word exam covers:

- Create and Manage Documents
- Format Text, Paragraphs, and Sections
- Create Tables and Lists
- Apply References
- Insert and Format Objects

The Excel exam covers:

- Create and Manage Worksheets and Workbooks
- Create Cells and Ranges
- Create Tables
- Apply Formulas and Functions
- Create Charts and Objects

The Outlook exam covers:

- Manage the Outlook Environment
- Manage Messages

- Manage Schedules
- Manage Contacts and Groups

The exams are all performance based with a project-like style – you need to build up an Office document or complete something according to the given specifications. There is a simulated environment for you to get your job done. To prepare for the exams, you need to know the various options available in the Office software. You know the options and functions available, then you can choose the right stuff and apply them in the correct order to achieve the project goal. **You must have hands-on experience!**

This ExamFOCUS book focuses on the more difficult topics that will likely make a difference in exam results. We introduce and explain the important options in the software that you cannot afford to miss. The book is NOT intended to guide you through every single step in the Office software. We assume that you already know the basics of using the graphical interface – you know the difference between single mouse click, double click, right click, drag and drop, press and hold …etc, and you know how to select and highlight text and objects. DO NOT TREAT THIS AS AN A-B-C GUIDE TO MS OFFICE. You should use this book together with other reference books for the best possible preparation outcome.

In the Office software you can usually achieve the same result using different methods. For example, once you highlighted some text you can either right click on the selection to access a small menu, or choose from the full blown menus (the ribbons) and toolbars at the top of the interface. Throughout the book we may use both methods for accessing functions and features. Also, keyboard shortcuts are available in the software but for exam prep purpose we will not use any of them unless required by the exams.

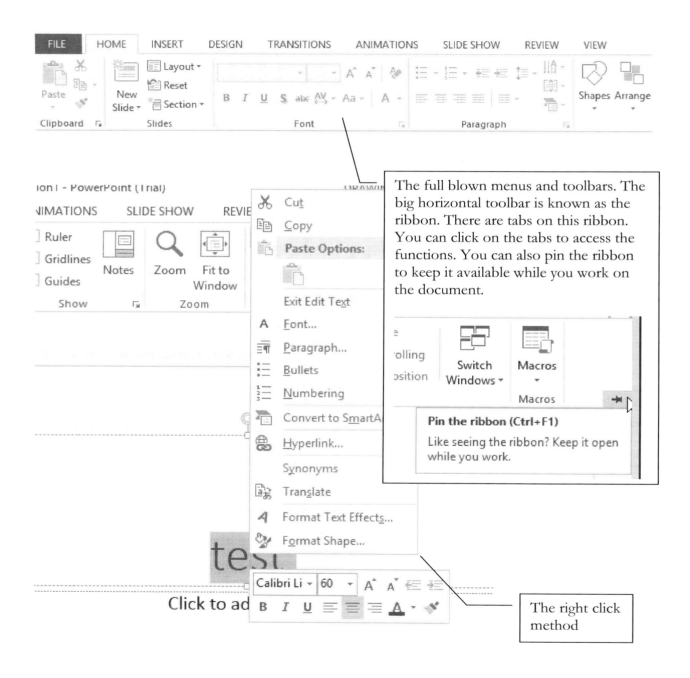

Preparing your trial installation

You should download the evaluation copy of Office 2013 Pro Plus and try things out for 60 days.

The download is in IMG format. You can use a CD burning software to burn the image into a CD media for installation and then run setup.exe to perform installation.

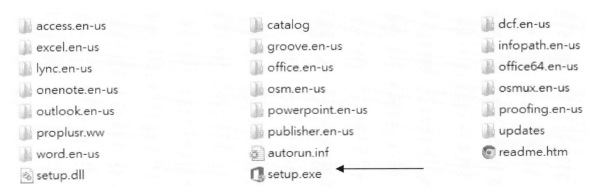

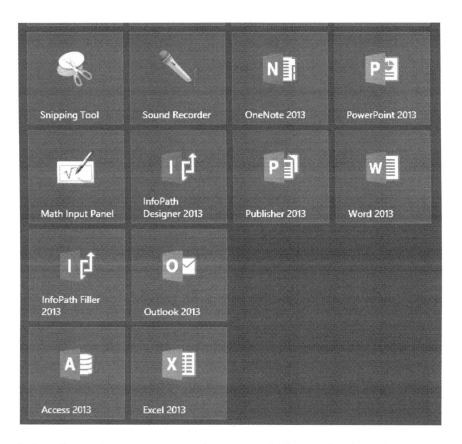

The first time you run it you will be asked to key in the product key. The key was provided to you at the time you download the software for evaluation.

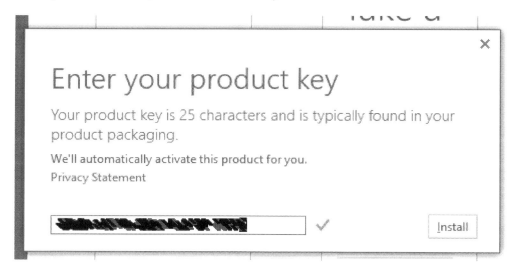

The primary Word interface

When you first start up Word you will be provided with this interface. Unless you are told to choose a particular template, you should click on Blank document to create a new file with nothing in it.

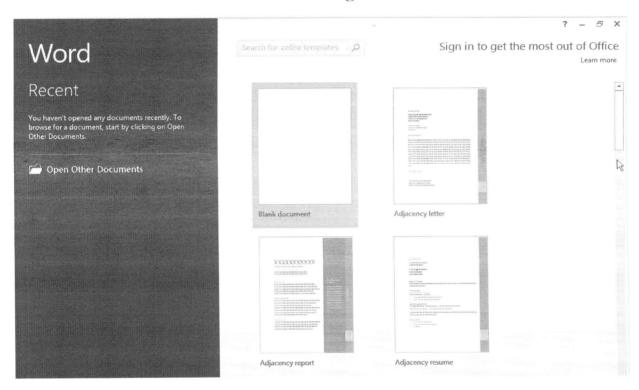

This is a blank document:

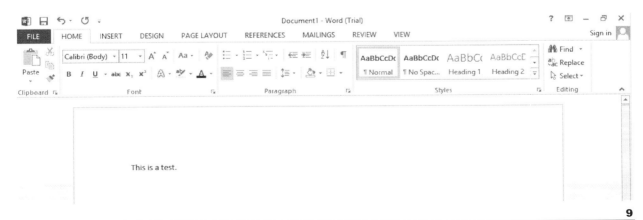

Home is where most text formatting functions are located.

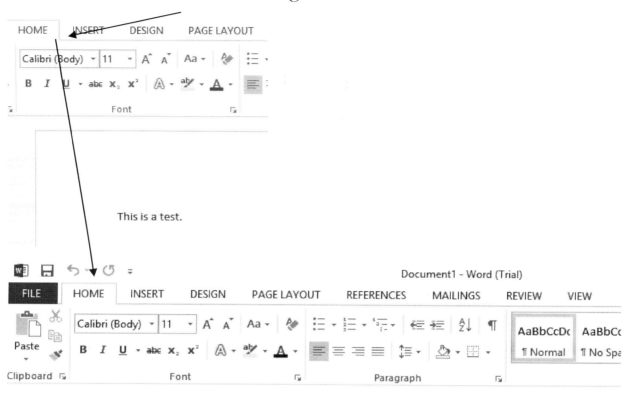

Most of the text formatting functions can be found on this HOME ribbon. We will deal with the various text formatting functions later in this book. On the left most part of the ribbon you can find the Clipboard, which allows you to perform cut and paste or copy and paste operations.

The VIEW ribbon allows you to change the view settings. View settings have nothing to do with the document itself. You may find it useful to enable the ruler. With the ruler displayed it is often easier to position tabs and change other paragraph settings.

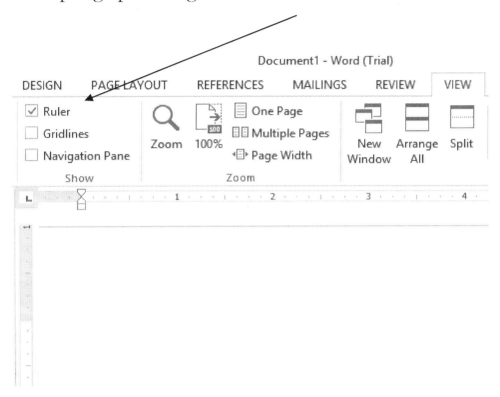

Word Documents

When you click on FILE you can access the File menu, which occupies the entire screen. If you click on the arrow button on the upper left corner you will switch back to the document view.

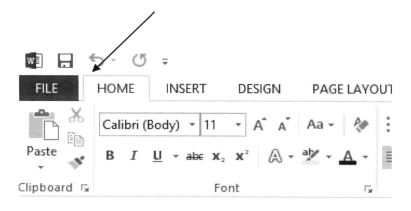

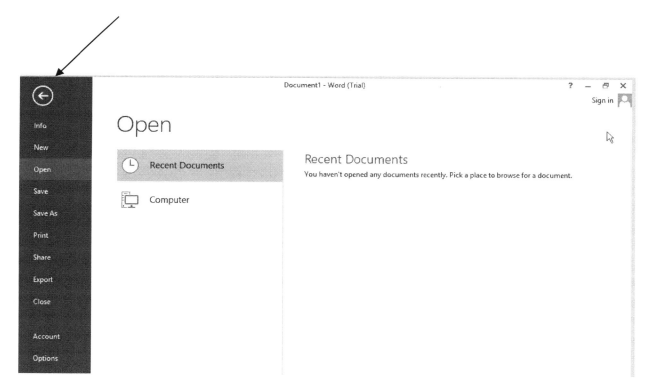

If you need to protect the document, Info is the section to visit. From there you can find "Protect Document".

Mark as final will make the document READ ONLY – no further changes will be accepted. To prevent unauthorized users from opening and viewing the document, you need to choose Encrypt with Password. The password you use is case sensitive. You should use a strong password that combines uppercase and lowercase letters, numbers, and symbols. You can have max 255 characters in your password.

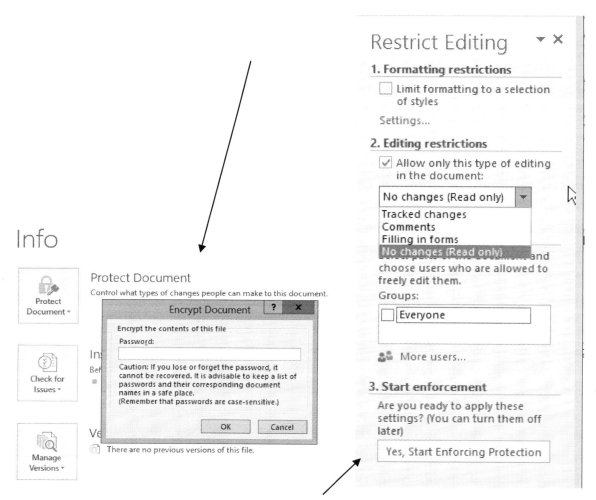

Formatting Restrictions is for protecting the document formatting. You can select the styles you want to allow and clear the styles you don't want to allow in the document. Restrict editing is not the same. It is about specifying the types of edit action to be prohibited. You must click on Start Enforcing

Protection for the restrictions to take effect. Restrict Access allows you to specify the user(s) who can open your file.

You may seal your document with a digital certificate, which means you digitally sign it. If you don't already have a digital certificate on your computer, you must first obtain one from somewhere. Word does not provide you with one.

Open allows you to pick an existing file to open. This file can be local or remote. A remote file is a file shared by another user on another computer. It can be opened only if you have been granted the necessary permissions.

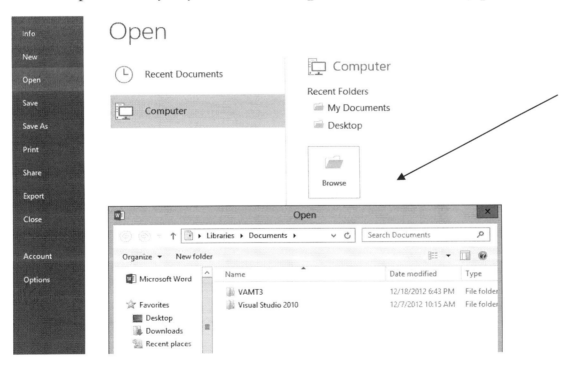

Save is different from Save As. If your file is already named, Save means saving the file without changing the file name and format. Save As gives you the chance to save the file data into a new one or even with a different format. Save As is a function primarily for compatibility – if you need to make the file available to users without Word 2013, you may need to save the file data using a different format. The default Word 2013 format is simply "Word Document".

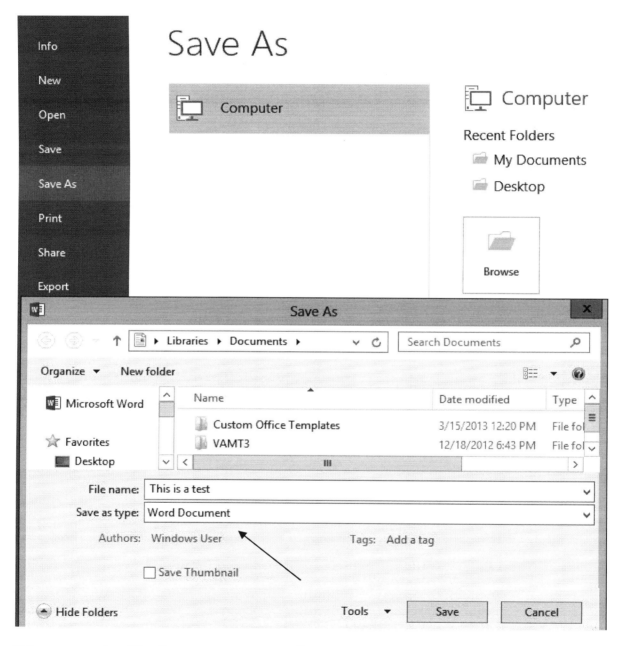

These are the file formats supported:

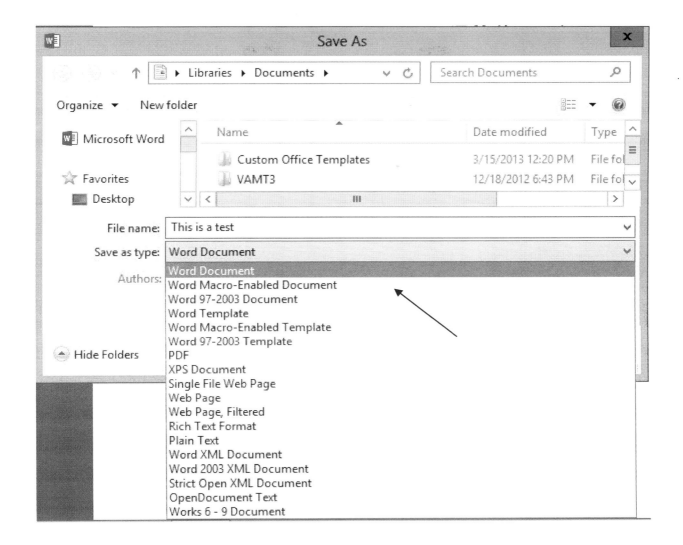

The Print section gives you a range of functions plus a print preview on the right. Printer allows you to pick the printer to use. Printer Properties are printer specific settings that have nothing to do with Word.

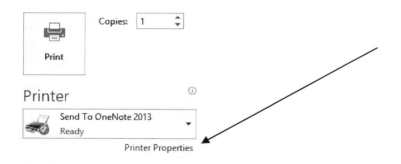

Settings

Settings are related to how you want your document to get printed. These are settings that are NOT printer specific. Most functions here are self-explanatory. You may want to use the Collated option if you are printing multiple copies of a multi-page document - this will ensure that your multi-page document is placed in complete sets that you can use immediately. Do note that if you select some pages or paragraphs and then change the orientation, Word will place the selected text on its own page and the other remaining text on separate pages, and will accordingly insert section breaks before and after the text with the new page orientation (this is how different orientations can survive in the same document).

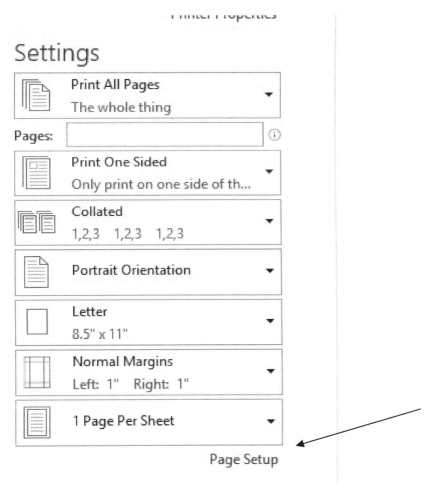

You can in fact click on Page Setup to fine tune page level settings such as page size and margins. Inside the Page Setup dialog box you can click on Print Options to access the Word Options screen. From there you can check the items that should be printed (hidden text, drawings, images …etc).

Print

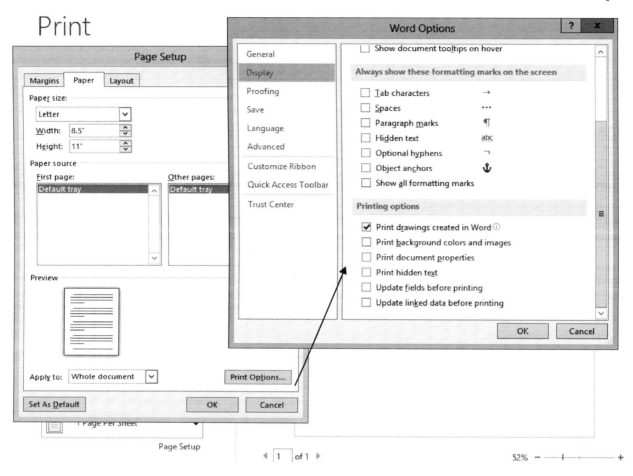

The best way to know these print options is to actually try them out! The last two options are related to database linking and are out of the scope of the exam.

The default setting allows you to print one document page per paper sheet. If you want to save paper and you don't mind to get smaller print output, you can choose to have multiple pages printed per sheet. Word will perform the scaling for you automatically.

Page Setup

Custom Print allows you to specify the page and section to print. P is page and S is section. For example, P1S2 means Page 1 Section 2. By default there is only one section throughout the document unless you manually insert section breaks in the document. You can think of a section as a unit that contains its own formatting. A section break is sort of an identifier that controls the section formatting elements that precedes it. Examples of these formatting elements include margins, paper size, page orientation, printer paper source, borders, text alignment, headers and footers, columns, page numbering, line numbering, footnotes and endnotes ...etc.

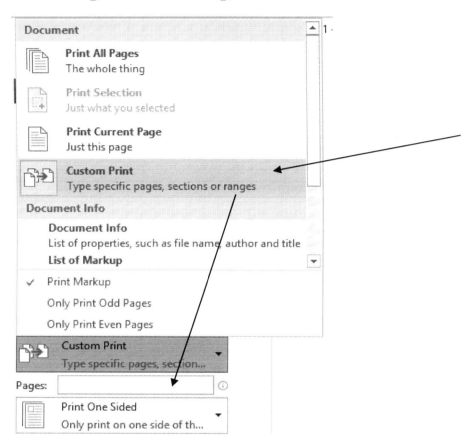

You can specify the range to print. Multiple ranges can be specified as long as you separate them with comma. For example, p1s1-p3s2, p8s4 – pp9s6

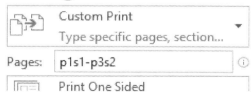

Share allows you to share this file with other people. Export allows you to create PDF and other documents out of it, which is similar to using SAVE AS.

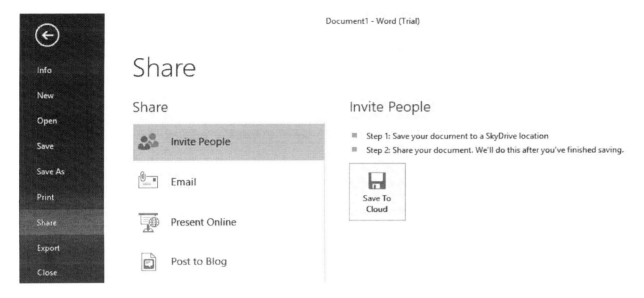

PDF is the way to go if you want to keep the file's format when you share it with other people. PDF file always looks the same on most computers. HOWEVER, Word cannot read nor edit a PDF file. It can only create one.

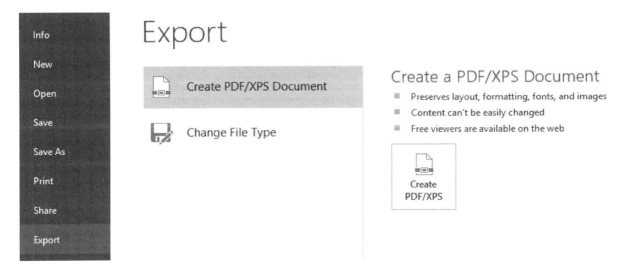

Options allows you to customize the various Word program features and interfaces. They are program level settings that should have nothing to do with the document you create.

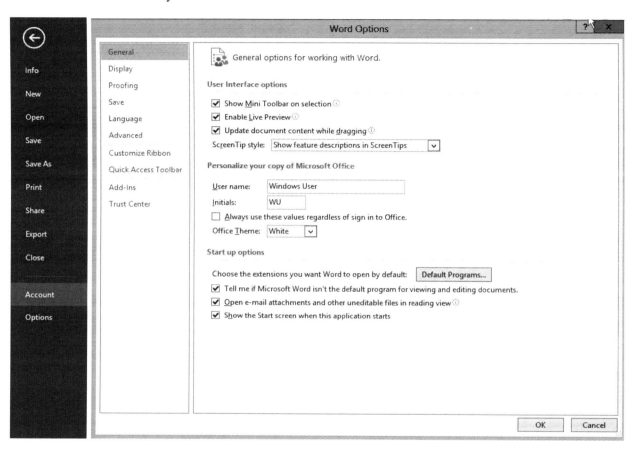

Word Document Formatting and Page Layout

Document level formatting can be done through Themes. Themes are like templates for the entire document – they have preset styles on every element of the document (color, text, background, layout …etc.). To be precise, a theme is a collection of formatting choices you can apply to an entire document. A style is a predefined combination of formatting choices specifically for fonts that can be applied to certain selected text but not to the entire document. You can access Themes via DESIGN. You can use preset themes and make changes as you see fit.

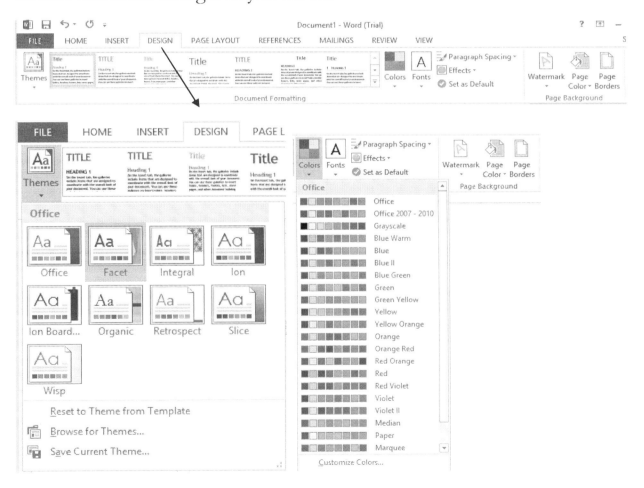

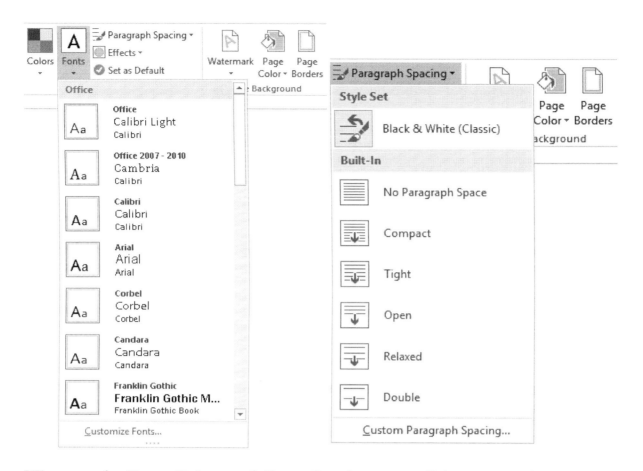

Watermark, Page Color and Page Borders can all be selected through the Page Background section:

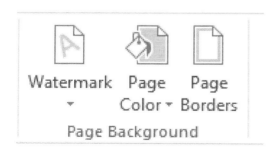

Do not forget – these are document level settings – they are supposed to apply to the entire document!

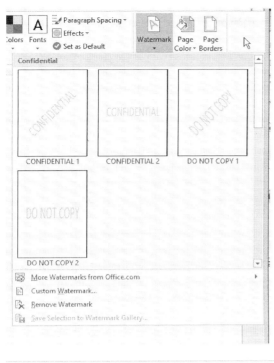
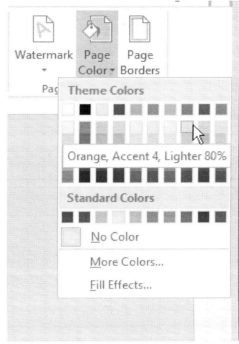
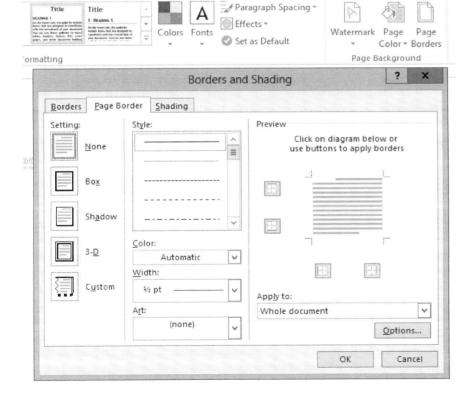

PAGE LAYOUT has options for page setup. If you click on the little icon at the lower right you can call up the Page setup screen. This is where you set margins, page orientation and paper size…etc without regard to the printer you use.

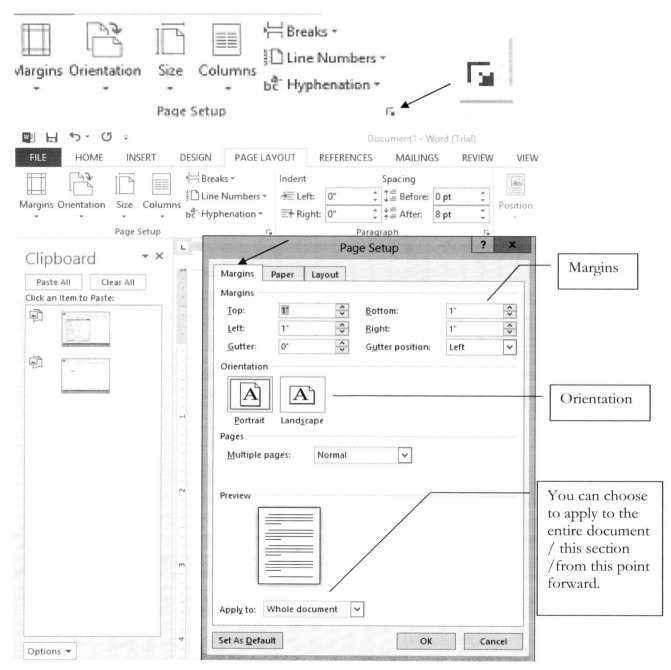

Changes on page setup can be applied on these scopes: Whole Document, This Point Forward, or This Section, even for paper size! There are standard paper sizes, or you can set width and height to create custom size page. Paper source is an option only for large scale laser printers with multiple different trays.

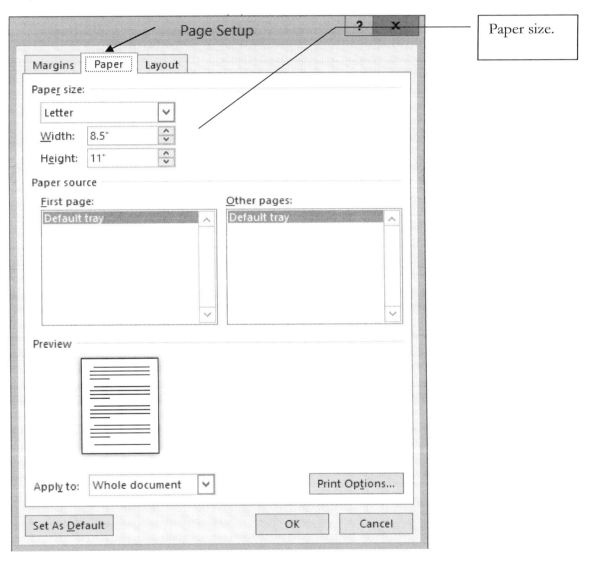

Headers and footers can be page level formatting if you choose to apply them to the whole document. They can also be section level formatting if you prefer to have different headers and footers in each section of your document. A typical way to change the headers and footers in different parts of a document is to insert a section break and then create a new section with its own headers and footers applied to this particular section. However, if you simply want a different header and footer for just the first page, simply click the Different First Page check box. The words "First Page Header" or "First Page Footer" will then appear in the upper left of the dashed Header or Footer box. Different odd and even is an option that works similarly and you should be able to tell its meaning based on its name!

The Line Numbers button can be used to call up the Line Numbers screen. You can configure Word to produce printable line numbering for the entire document. Line numbering is particularly useful in legal documents. Note the numbering options available, which are Restart each page, Restart each section and Continuous.

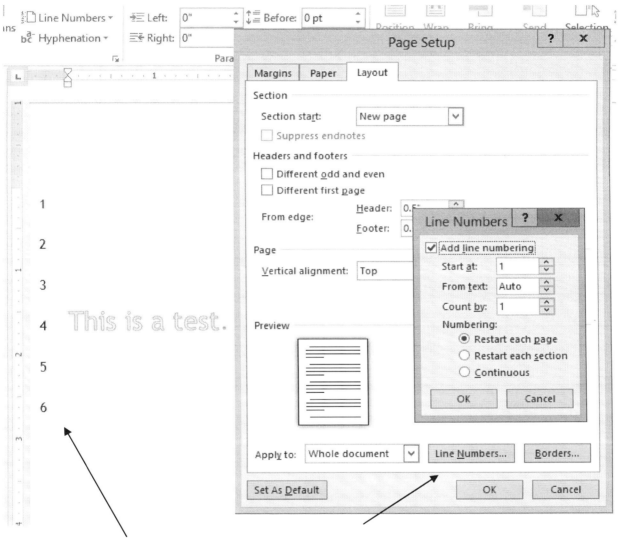

For your information, header and footer can also be inserted into the document through the INSERT ribbon - if you do it through INSERT you can select from a range of built-in styles. To add a page number, click Page

Number and choose Top of Page or Bottom of Page. Choose Format Page Numbers to pick a number format that fits your need.

If you want to create a cover page for your document, go to INSERT and select Cover Page. There are ready made cover pages available.

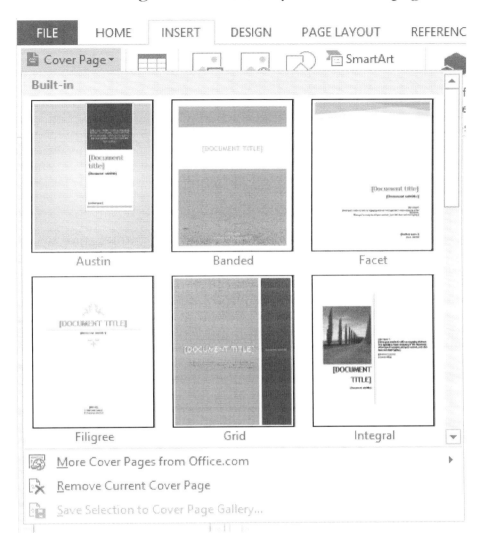

After inserting a cover page, you should replace the default sample text by clicking on an area of the cover page that holds the sample text and typing in your own text. Also, if you insert another cover page, the new cover page will replace the original cover page that you inserted before.

Text Formatting and Lists in Word

Whenever you want to change the formatting and style of your text, you should select the text first. After that, from the HOME ribbon you click to open the different formatting dialog boxes.

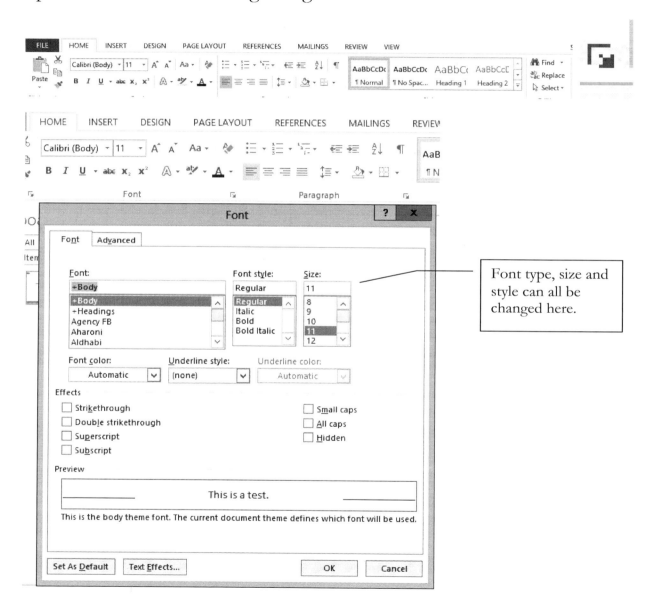

Font type, size and style can all be changed here.

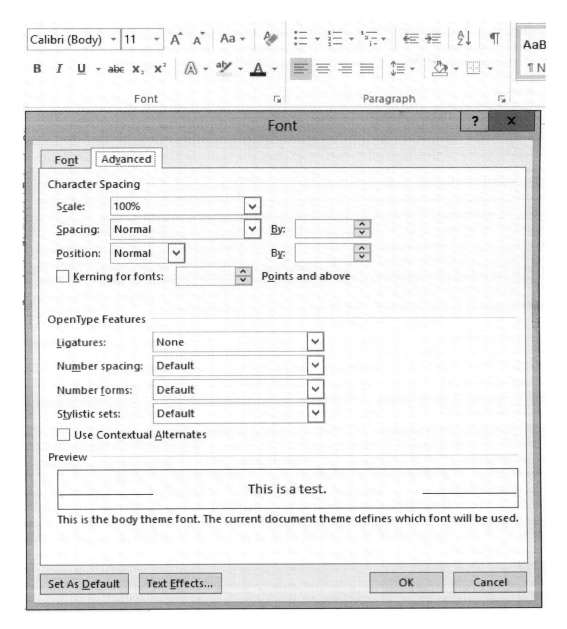

All the font related options are pretty much self-explanatory. On the other hand, if you simply want to change text alignment (the default is left), use this toolbar:

Text Effects produces graphical effects for your text, such as special color, text outline and transparency effects. You are encouraged to try them out on your own.

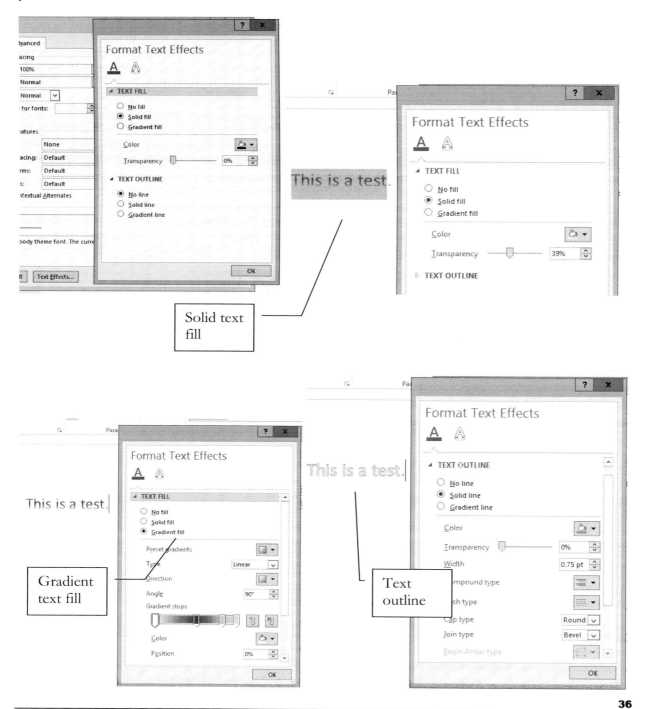

A list can be bulleted or numbered. On the HOME ribbon you can find a tab that shows the lists. First highlight the pieces of text that are supposed to form your list, then click the tab and choose a list format.

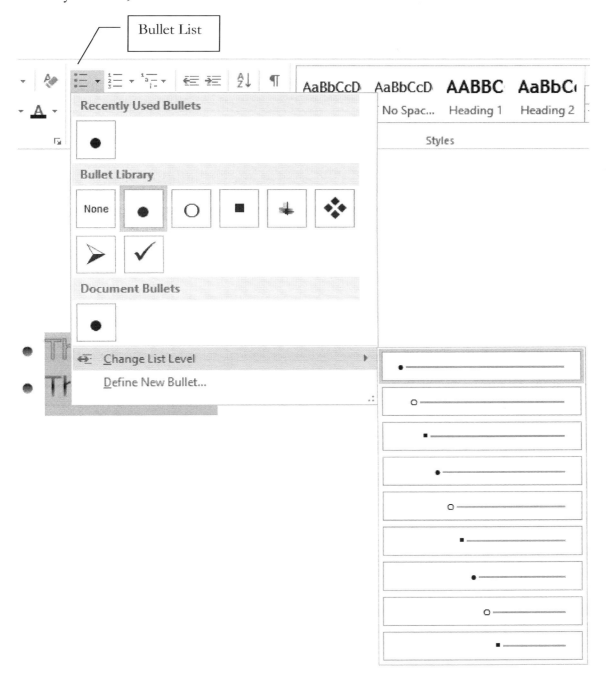

Change List level allows you to change the selected list item(s) to a different level. You can also click Define New Bullet to come up with your own bullet design. For numbered list you can make your own numbering format.

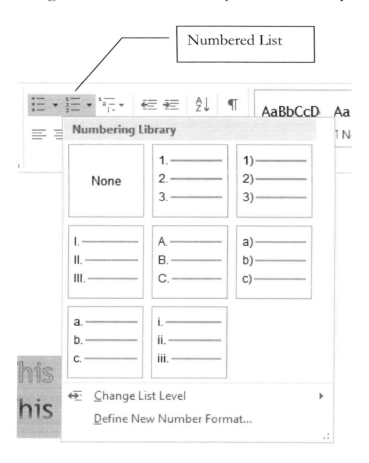

A multilist item allows you to produce a multilevel list that shows the list items at different levels. If the multilevel list styles available do not fit your need, you can create and define a new one via Define New Multilevel List. FYI, if you use Define New List Style to create a new list style and then you make changes to this style, every instance of this list style will get updated in the document. This won't happen with Define New Multilevel List. Define New Multilevel List is more for quick and convenient use at a single place.

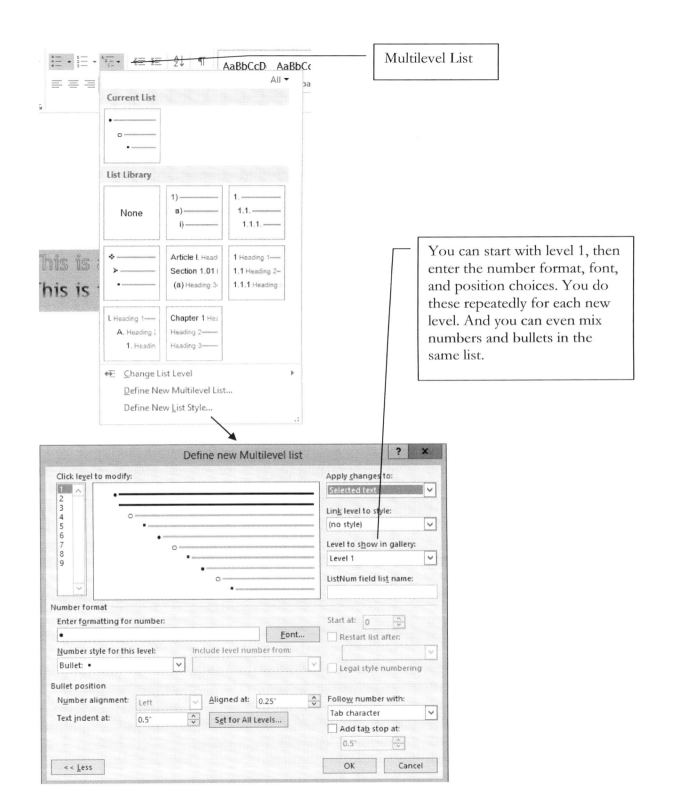

You want to know how to use the format painter, which is represented by the little brush like icon.

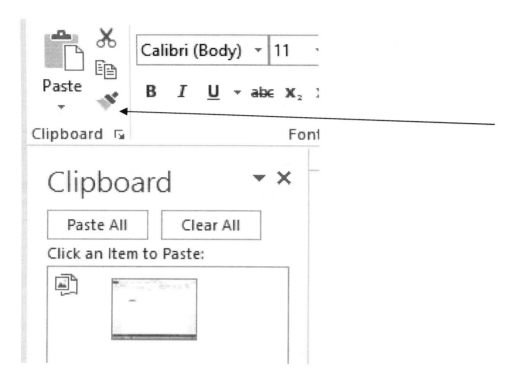

It is for copying the formatting of text. To use it, first select the text that has the formatting to be copied. Then click on it, and then click the text you want to format. Along the process your mouse cursor will be changed to a brush like shape.

Paragraphs and Sections in Word

Before working with paragraph formatting you want to enable the display of all paragraph formatting marks. Without seeing these marks it will be difficult to make accurate placement and positioning. The default is to keep these marks hidden, which may not be preferable. From the FILE ribbon you go into Options – Word Options - Display. From there you can pick the proper options:

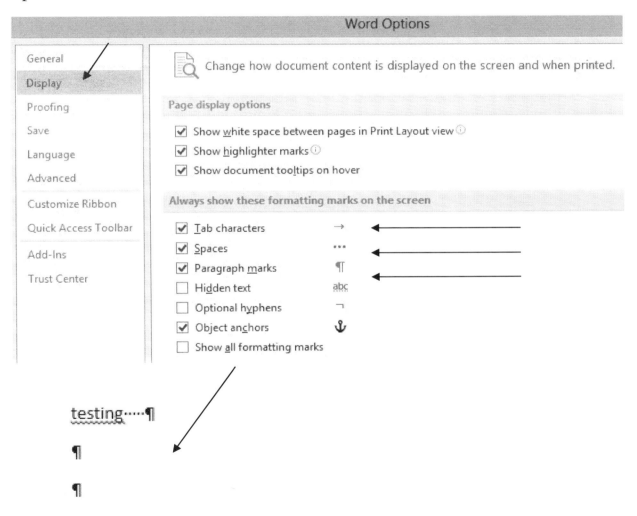

The Paragraph screen provides you with options to change alignment, indentation and line spacing at the paragraph level. In any case you should first select the paragraph(s) that you want to change.

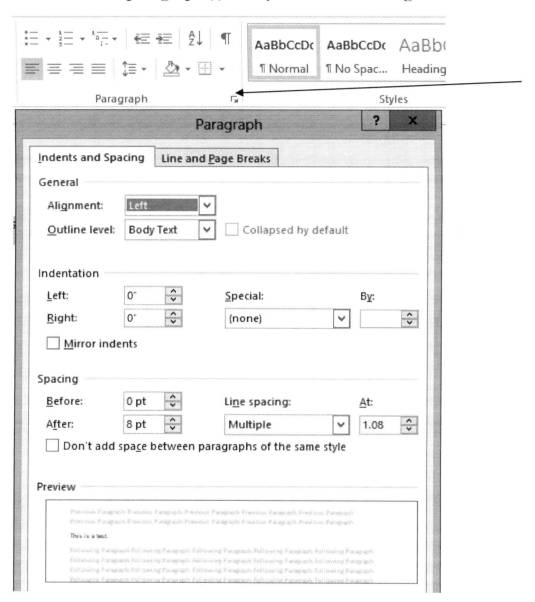

Indentation is all about setting the distance of the paragraph from the left or the right margin (normally from the left). With these special margins in place you may increase or reduce the indentation of your paragraph(s) as needed. It is also possible to create a negative indent (which is effectively an outdent) or a hanging indent (only the first line of a paragraph is not indented). Line spacing is all about inserting extra space between all lines of text in a paragraph. If you choose Exactly or At least for line spacing, you will need to enter the amount of space you want in the At box.

Tab stops help you align or indent your text. They appear on the horizontal ruler if you have ruler enabled via VIEW. You may manually key in the desired tab stop position. You can have multiple tab stops on a line. Once the tab stops are in place, you can use the keyboard Tab key to move text accordingly.

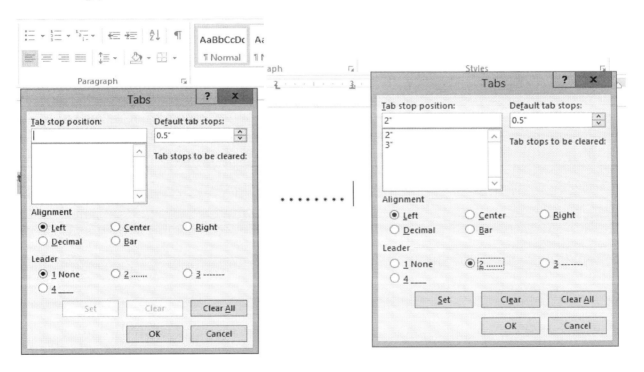

The Line and Page Breaks section has many pagination options that deserve your attention.

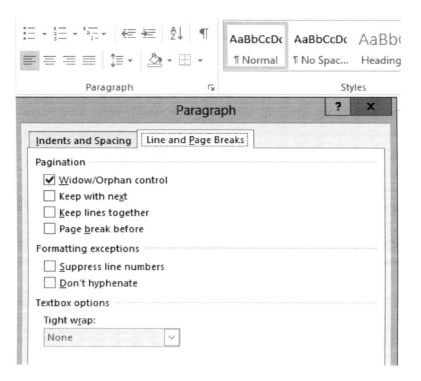

Widow/Orphan Control is an option that allows a paragraph to split across two pages. This option explicitly disallows any single line of paragraph from dangling by itself at page top or bottom. Either the last two lines of the paragraph will be shown at the top of the following page, or that the entire paragraph will be pushed to the new page. Keep lines together works the opposite - it maintains the entire paragraph on a single page whenever possible, disallowing the splitting of a paragraph across pages. With Keep with next, Word always keeps a paragraph in close proximity to its subsequent paragraph. Page break before is an option that always insert a page break before a paragraph - it is just like using the keyboard shortcut "Ctrl Enter". Text boxes are containers that allow you to control the position of blocks of text. In theory you can place text boxes anywhere and format them with either nothing or special shading and borders. We will deal with text boxes later in this book.

You can insert page break into your document via the INSERT ribbon. The break goes right after your current cursor position. Other break types can be dealt with via the PAGE LAYOUT ribbon. The available options are pretty much self-explanatory. Next Page is a session break that inserts a new page or continues text on the next consecutive page. Continuous is a session break that starts a new section without adding a page. Even Page is a session break that inserts a new even-numbered page or continues your text only on the next even-numbered page. Odd Page is a session break that inserts an odd-numbered new page or continues your text only on the next odd-numbered page.

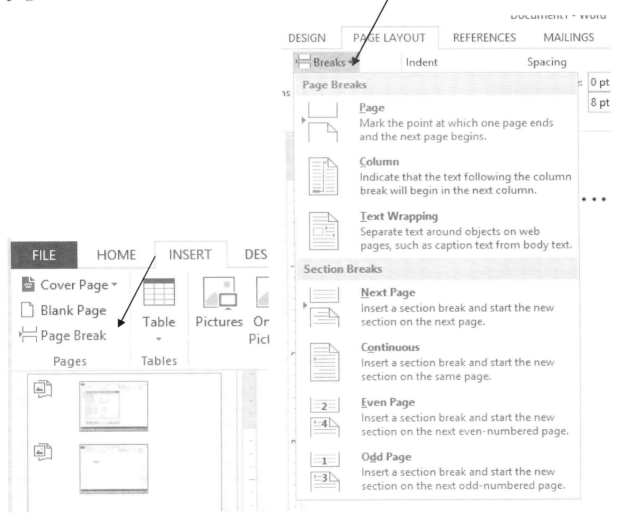

Removing a break is easy. Make sure the break is clearly displayed. Place your cursor right before the break and then press the DEL key.

Hyphenation is useful when you always have words that are too long to fit on the end of a line. Without this feature, Word will simply move a long word to the beginning of the next line. With this feature, Word will insert hyphen into the word, which can eliminate gaps in the justified text. When you use automatic hyphenation, Word will automatically inserts hyphens whenever they are needed. With manual hyphenation, Word will ask you for confirmation first.

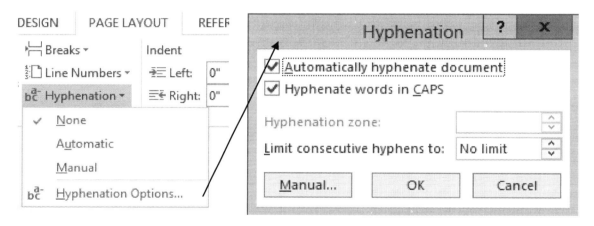

Hyphenate Words in CAPS means words in all caps can be hyphenated. This setting is often used when there are a lot of jargons or trade names in the document. Limit consecutive hyphens to is all about limiting the number of consecutive lines Word should hyphenate. Having too many at a time may look strange!

Tables in Word

These tables are NOT the TOC (Table of Contents) tables. They are just tables for laying out text and/or graphics. You can set borders and shading for them, or you can keep them transparent. You use the INSERT ribbon to insert a new table – from the menu you can quickly "draw" a new table by dragging over the cells:

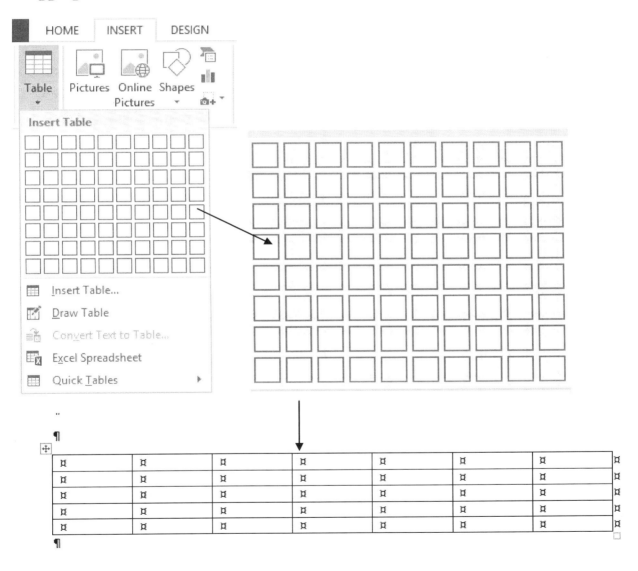

Or, you can choose to insert a Quick Table, which is pre-built table with all the formatting already in place.

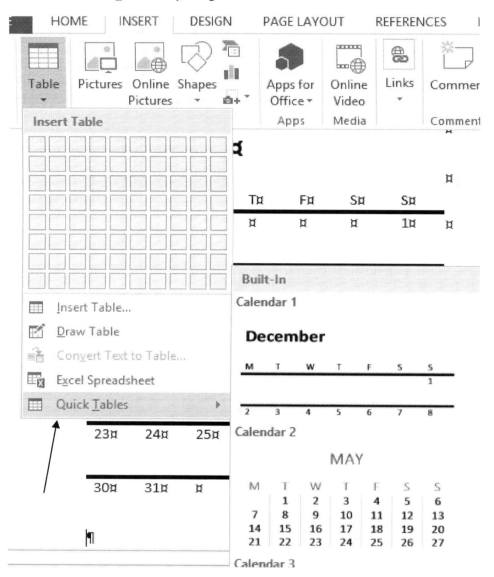

To change the formatting of an existing table, click on the upper left corner to select the entire table, and you will see a popup menu. From there you can choose to set the border and shading. You can also directly drag on the table column/row/cell to change their size.

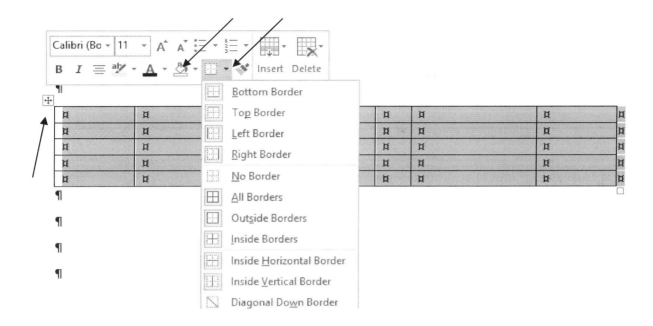

If you accidentally change the cell size and you want to restore to the default, simply right click on the table and choose Distribute Rows/Columns Evenly.

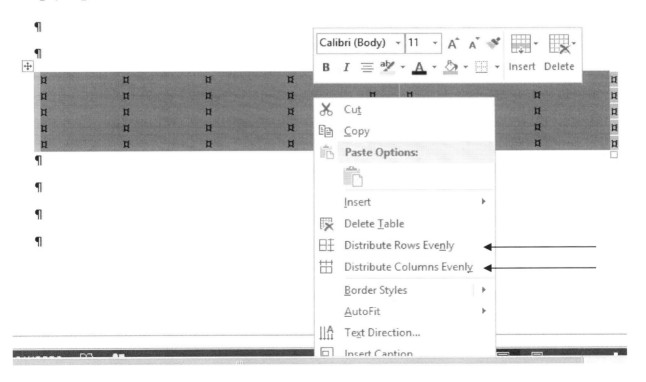

References in Word

Table of Content TOC requires that you first select text pieces from your document as headings. You can have many levels of heading but most of the time you want to use no more than 3 levels.

You select a piece of text and then go to HOME and click Styles, or simply click on the drop down list and quickly pick a heading style.

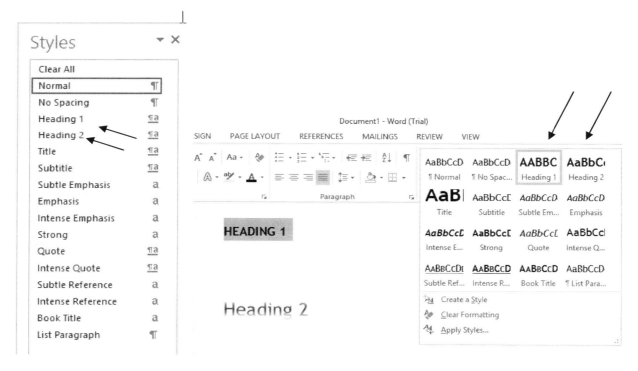

To create a new TOC, first place your cursor on the desired page, then go to the REFERENCES ribbon and click Table of Contents. You can choose a predefined format (Automatic Table) or make a custom one via Custom Table of Contents. A custom table allows you to add or reduce heading levels as well as to change the different styles involved.

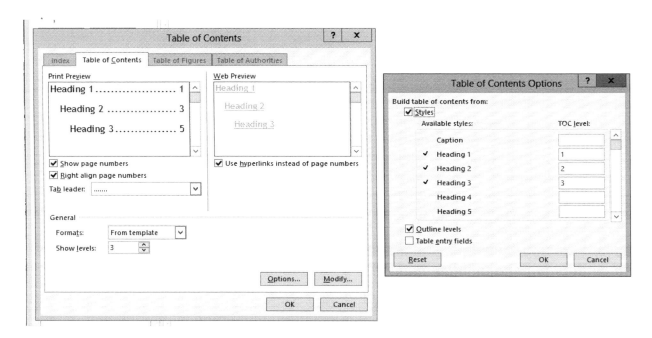

When the actual contents are updated (for example, new contents added, contents moved or changed …etc), you can right click on the TOC and choose Update Field to update the TOC (so the TOC can reflect the latest changes in the contents).

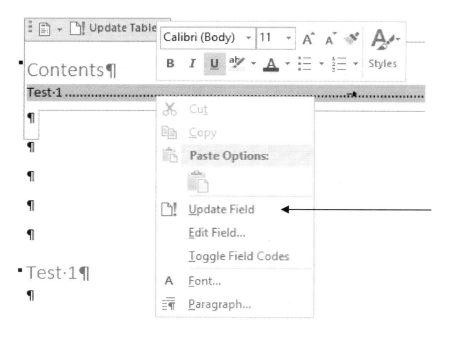

To create an Index, you also need to mark the indexed words or phrases from the content text first. Select a text piece, then choose REFERENCES – Mark Entry. From the Mark Index Entry dialog box you click Mark. You need to mark the desired text pieces from the document one by one. Click Close when you are done.

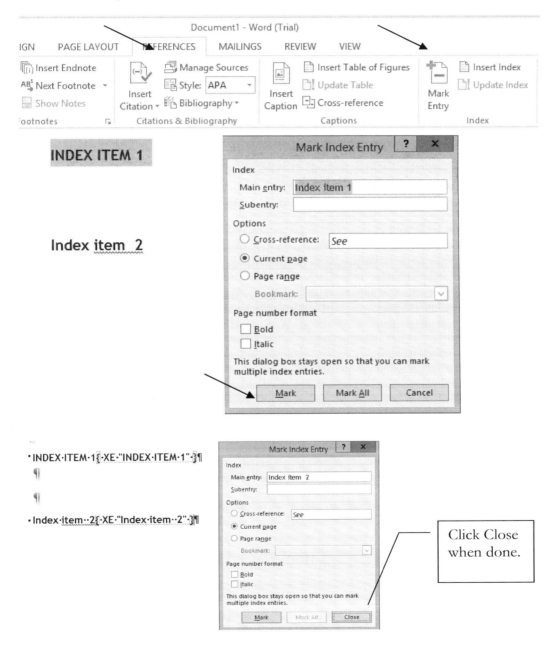

Note that you can always highlight an abbreviation to include in your index and then edit the Main Entry field to include the full spelling of the word. When you finish marking the index items, you can place your cursor in the desired location and choose REFERENCES – Insert Index to place the index over there. To replace an existing index, simply place your cursor over it and insert a new one.

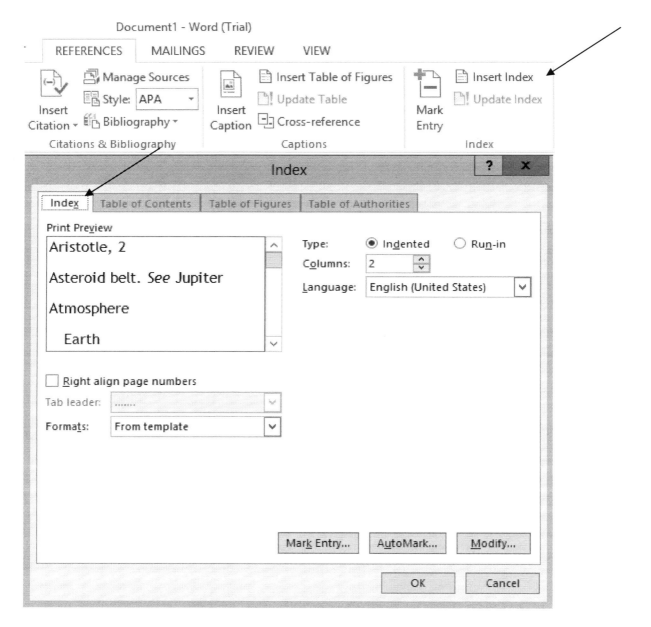

You want to check the Right Align Page Numbers option if you want the index page numbers to be placed at the right most side of the index. Tab Leader refers to the dotted line that connects the index entry to its page number. AutoMark is special - you first create a file known as an Index AutoMark file. You then instruct Word to use this file to identify all text pieces that should be marked as index items. Simply put, this is an advanced automation feature not likely to be used by regular users.

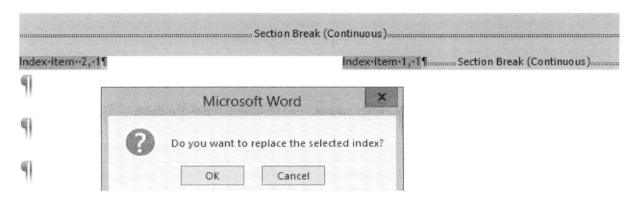

A cross-reference is different - you use it to cross-references within the document text to refer from one part of the document to another. You can manually type in the reference:

Bibliography, Endnotes, Footnotes and Captions in Word

A bibliography is a list of sources and works cited. You usually have it placed at the end of your document. When you add a new citation, you are effectively creating a new source, which is like a database record of the work cited. First place your cursor in the appropriate place of your document. Then, from REFERENCES, you click Insert Citation and choose Add New Source. Fill in the information and click OK, then Word will create a source field in the document for you. The field can be edited at any time by clicking on it and choose the proper option. Keep in mind, the process of adding citations cannot be automated – you have to create them one by one. If you do not have the source information yet, add a placeholder instead.

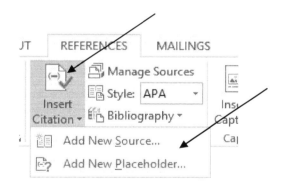

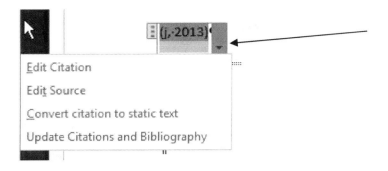

To create the bibliography, place your cursor in the proper location and then click Bibliography. Pick a style from the drop down menu. Bibliography, References and Works Cited all mean the same thing here.

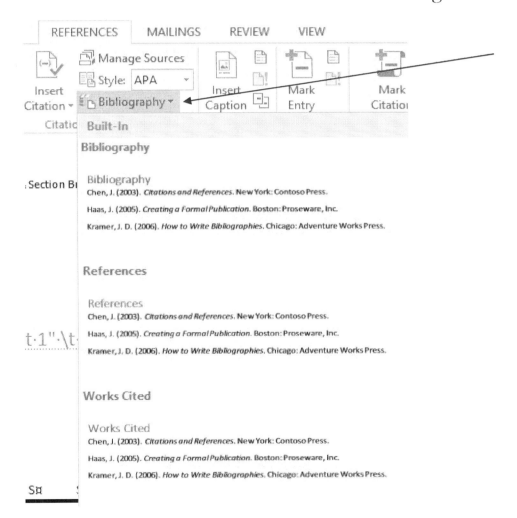

The bibliography will then be generated automatically.

- Bibliography¶
  j, m. (2013). *testing book.* sj: examreview.¶

  ¶

You can use footnotes and/or endnotes to comment on text in your document. Most of the time people prefer to use footnotes for detailed comments and endnotes for giving references. You go to REFERENCES and click Insert Footnote to place one at the bottom of the page. Numbering is automatic but the note content must be keyed in by yourself.

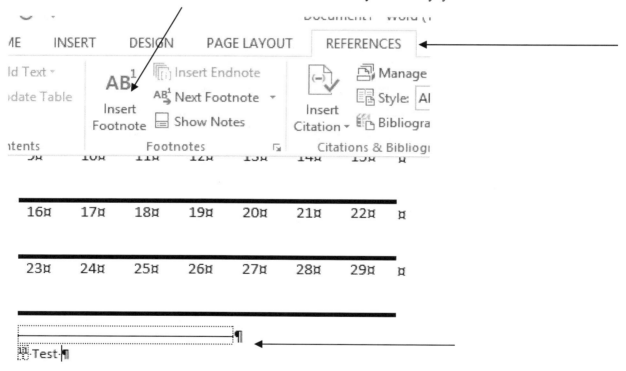

You can also choose to Insert Endnote. The difference is that footnote is available at the bottom of every page while endnote is an end of section/end of document feature. You can change the settings via this dialog box:

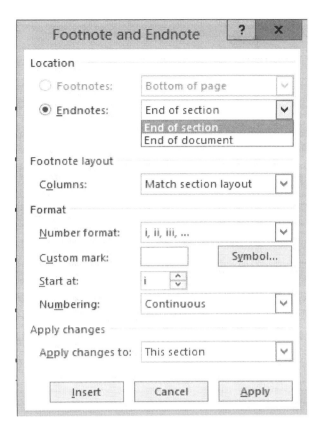

Captions are for labeling figures and drawings. You go to REFERENCES and click Insert Caption to insert a caption into the current cursor position. You then fill in the information. Note that this caption will correspond to an entry in the Table of Figures.

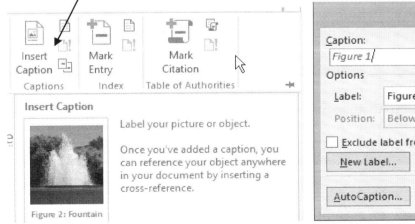
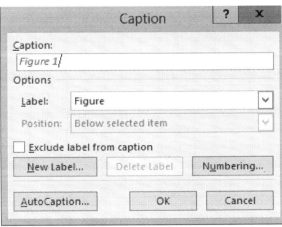

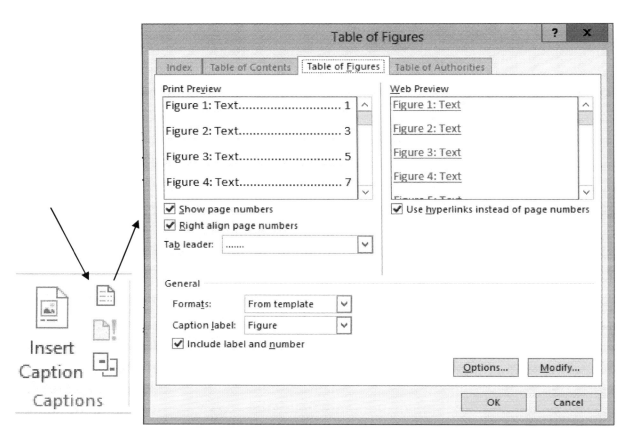

Technically, you can add captions to figures, equations, or any other kinds of object in the document. If you are specifically told to use a particular style for the table, click Options and choose Style, then pick a style from the drop down list.

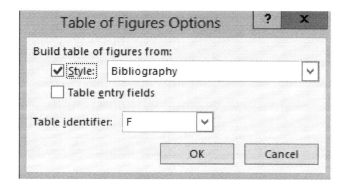

Building Blocks, Quick Parts, Shapes, Pictures and others

Technically, anything selectable in Word can be made as part of a Building Block. Building Blocks are predefined document content pieces glued together and saved for future use. They usually contain multiple paragraphs of text, tables, lists, or other content types. Word comes with many predefined Building Blocks, such as headers, footers, cover pages, text boxes, equations ...etc. To create a building block, select the components you have created in your document, then choose INSERT - Text Box - Save Selection to Quick Part Gallery. This will call up a special dialog box.

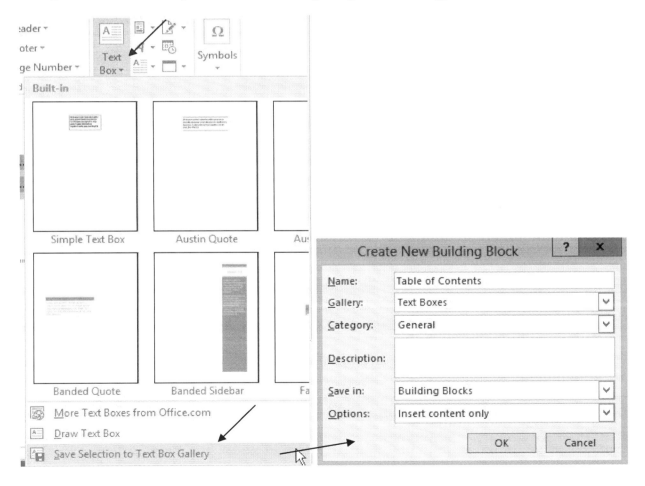

By default, all new Building Blocks you add will be categorized as General. You may create a new category as you see fit. Once this building block is saved, you can always retrieve and use it as a Quick Part. The Building Blocks Organizer is an interface that provides a comprehensive list of all the available building blocks in the current template. Through it you can see the building block name, the gallery type, the category and other information. You can even use it to modify, insert, or delete individual building block entries. You may invoke this interface via the Explore Quick Parts button:

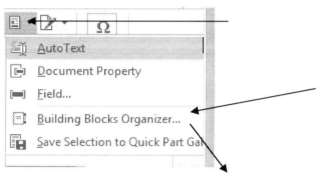

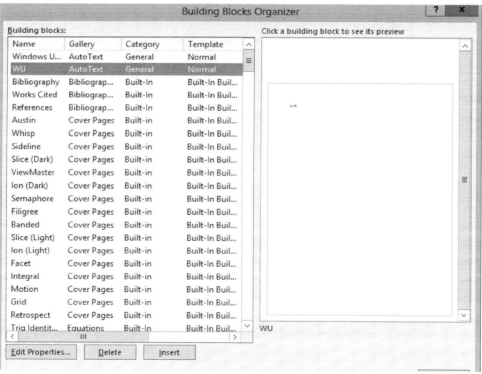

Instead of inserting a building block, you can simply insert a text box. The key to using a text box is specifying how it is to be positioned in the document. When you choose to insert a text box, you simply drag it into the document and you may manipulate it freely.

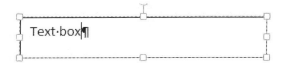

If you right click on it, you can actually change the wrap text settings:

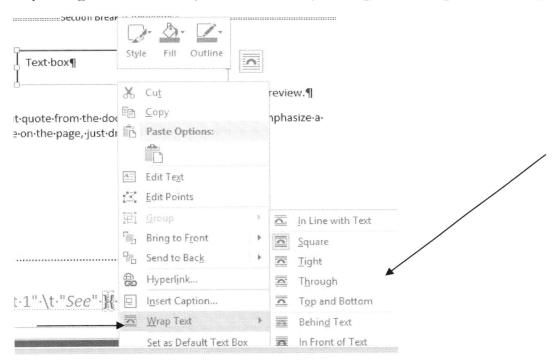

Keep in mind, these wrap text settings are available for text boxes and also for all other Word objects such as drawings, shapes, WordArts …etc. The best way to learn how these settings differ is for you to try them out yourself! By default an inserted object is free floating – you can position it freely via dragging. To disallow object free floating you will need to set it to stay in line with text. *Do note that rotation is possible only if free floating is allowed.*

In line with text is the default setting. Square means your text will flow around the object or image. Tight means the margins between the object/image and your text will get smaller. Top and bottom means your text will appear at the top and bottom of the object/image. Behind text means your object/image will appear behind your text, effectively becoming a background image. In front of text does the exact opposite.

You can insert a foreign application object such as an Excel spreadsheet or PowerPoint slide into the document via INSERT – Object. You can create a new instance of such foreign object or import from an existing file.

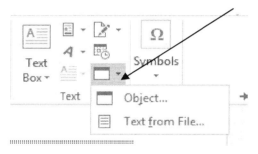

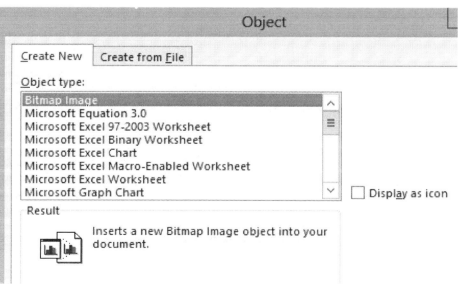

Ready-made shapes can be chosen from INSERT – Shapes. WordArt items can be created through INSERT – Insert WordArt.

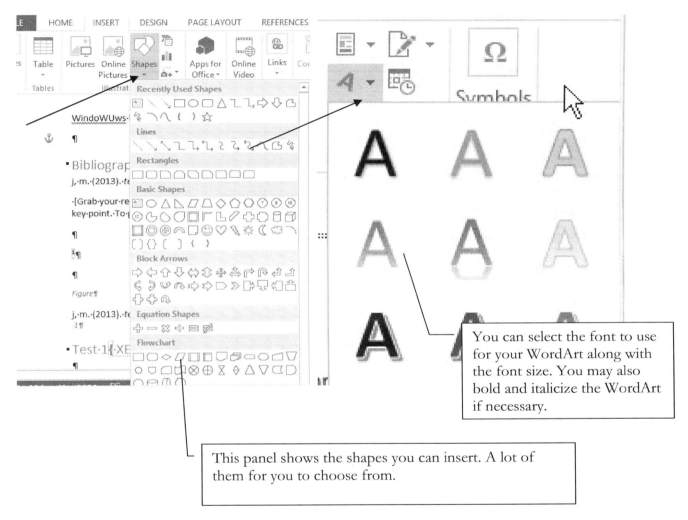

Once a shape is inserted into your document, you can click to select it and make its resize handles visible at each corner and along each edge. You can click and drag on anyone of those to resize the shape. You can also keep the shape's proportions by only dragging the corner handle. You can even squash the shape by dragging a handle along the edge. Note that the green rotation handle at the top can be used to rotate the shape anticlockwise or clockwise.

Bitmap images can be inserted via INSERT – Pictures. Popular image formats like BMP, JPG and GIF are all supported.

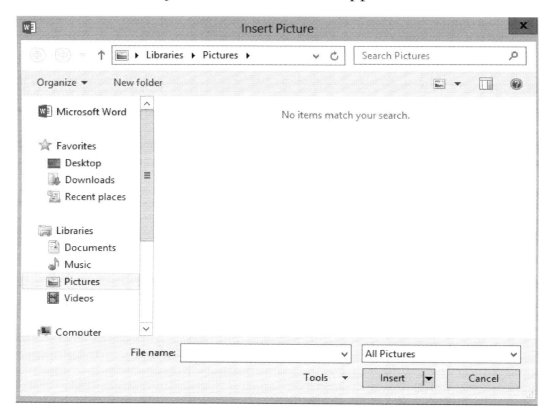

Once an object is placed inside a document, you can always right click on it to access its menu. More Layout Options allows you to precisely set the object's position and layout by keying in numerical measurements. Format Shape allows you to set color fill, line style and other special effects such as shadow, glow and reflection.

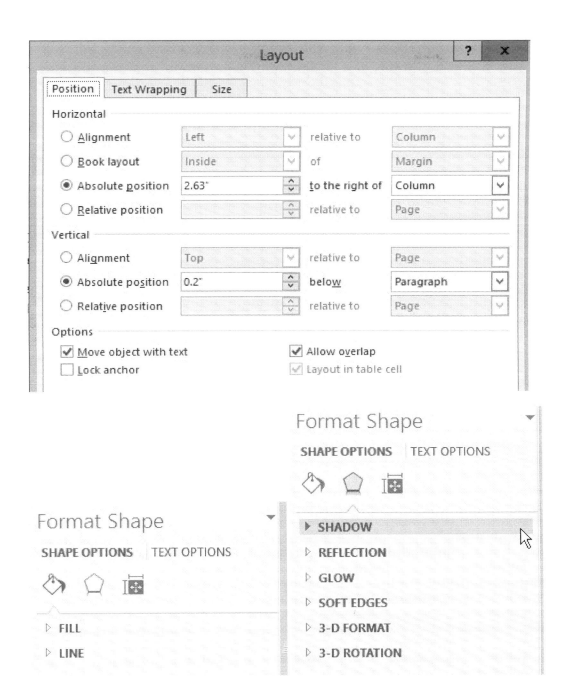

When you draw a shape, you usually do not like the default fill color. You can always change the shape's fill to be a different color or a gradient - a fill that shows a color merging smoothly into another. You can pick two colors to form the gradient fill.

Macro and Shortcut Keys in Word

Macros is an automation feature for automating your frequently performed tasks. A macro records what you have done and replays your actions. On the right-most part of the VIEW ribbon you can find Macros. Click on it and choose Record Macro to record a new one.

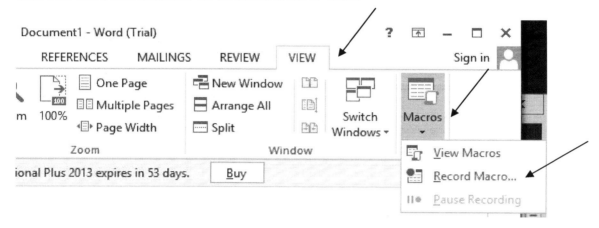

You may want to assign the macro to, say, a shortcut key combination so you can easily call it up. Assigning to a button involves changing the interface a little bit and you may want to skip this for now.

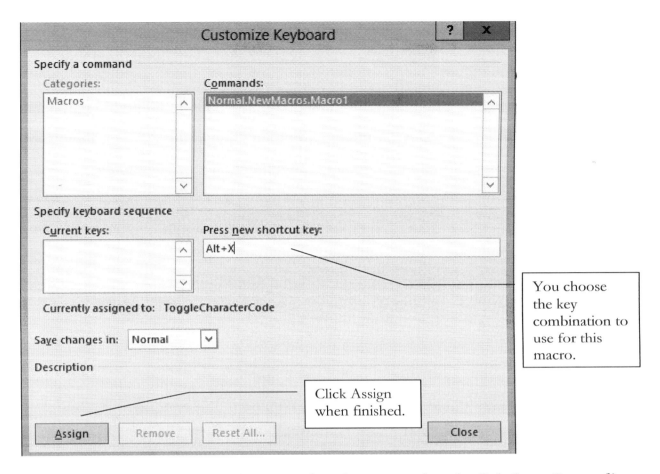

Now you may do your work as usual. When completed, click Stop Recording.

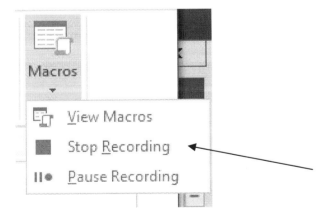

Now the macro is saved in the list of macros. You can either use the short cut key combination to run it, or simply select it and click Run.

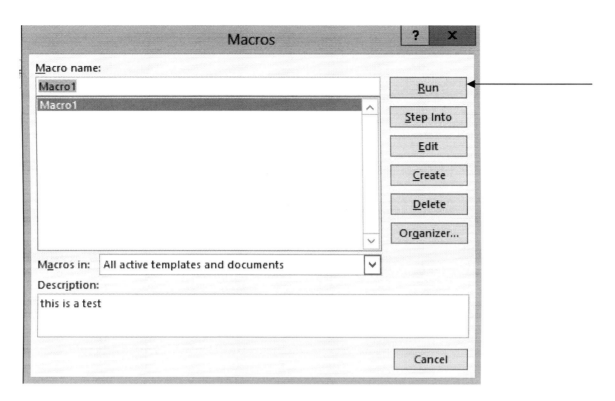

If you click Edit you will go into the VBA (Visual Basic for Application) coding mode, which is way beyond the scope of regular word processing.

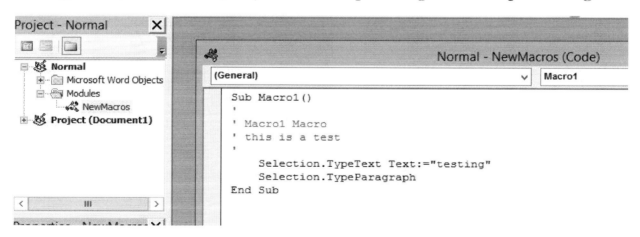

Since macro can be coded, it is possible for a destructive macro to spread like a virus. Macro security is something to be configured in the Trust Center, which is located at FILE – Options – Word Options – Trust Center – Trust Center Settings.

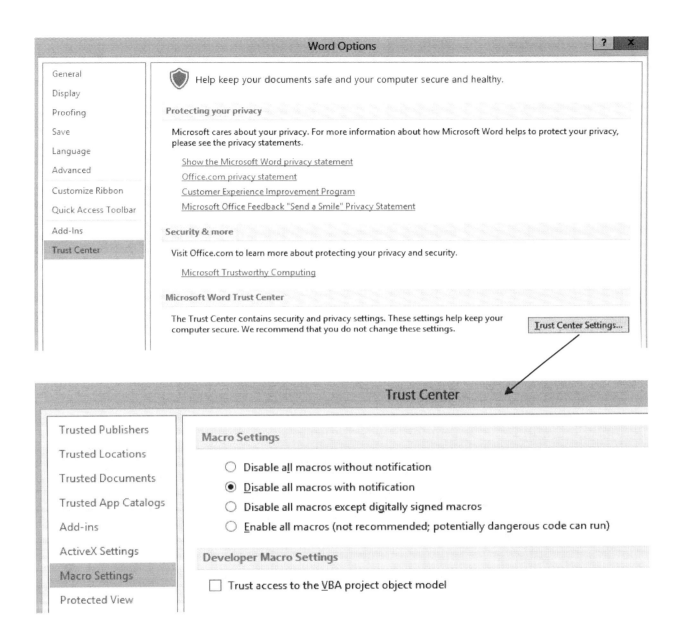

The default is Disable all macros with notification, which means macros are disabled but you will get security alerts when there are macros present so you can choose when to enable macros again. Disable all macros except digitally signed macros is similar but macros digitally signed by a trusted publisher can automatically run. Enable all macros means all macros can run without alerts, which can be quite unsafe!

The primary Excel interface

When you first start up Excel you will be provided with this interface. Unless you are told to choose a particular template, you should click on Blank workbook to create a new file with nothing in it.

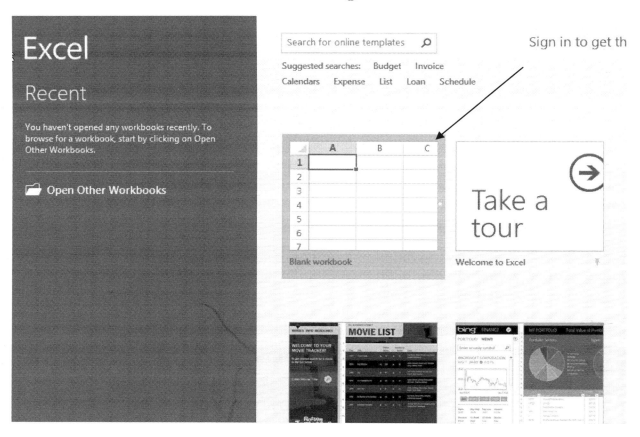

HOME is where most text formatting functions are located.

Most of the text formatting functions can be found on this HOME ribbon. We will deal with the various text formatting functions later in this book. You must realize that in Excel, the focus is more on setting the calculation functions. You will see need to deal with formatting, just that more attention will be paid to the calculation and chart creation aspects of the software.

This is a blank spreadsheet:

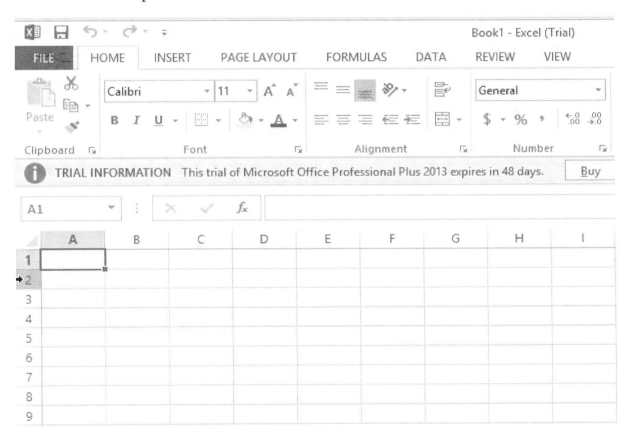

On the left most part of the HOME ribbon you can find the Clipboard, which allows you to perform cut and paste or copy and paste operations. Excel does have many special paste functions!

The VIEW ribbon allows you to change the view settings. View settings have nothing to do with the spreadsheet itself. Excel does have several workbook views available. The default is the Normal view.

The Page Layout View shows the content as it would appear on a printed page. The Page Break Preview shows the worksheet content as it would appear over multiple pages. You may also define custom views although this is usually not required by the exam.

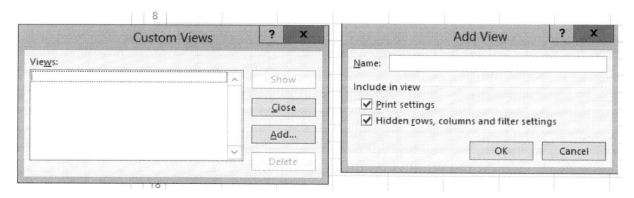

Worksheets and Workbooks

A workbook is the entire Excel file. A worksheet is a single spreadsheet within this file. Each workbook can have many worksheets. However, you should have only one theme for each workbook for the sake of consistency across the file.

When you click on FILE you can access the File menu, which occupies the entire screen. If you click on the arrow button on the upper left corner you will switch back to the spreadsheet view.

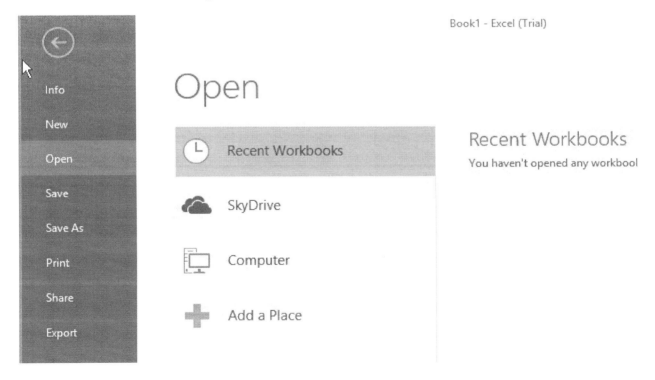

If you need to protect the spreadsheet, Info is the section to visit. From there you can find a number of protection options within the Protect Workbook section.

Book1 - Excel (Trial)

Info

Protect Workbook
Control what types of changes people can make to this workbook.

Inspect Workbook
Before publishing this file, be aware that it contains:
- Author's name and absolute path

Versions
There are no previous versions of this file.

Browser View Options
Pick what users can see when this workbook is viewed on the Web.

Info

Protect Workbook
Control what types of changes people can make to this workbook.

Mark as Final
Let readers know the workbook is final and make it read-only.

Encrypt with Password
Require a password to open this workbook.

Protect Current Sheet
Control what types of changes people can make to the current sheet.

Protect Workbook Structure
Prevent unwanted changes to the structure of the workbook, such as adding sheets.

Restrict Access
Grant people access while removing their ability to edit, copy, or print.

Add a Digital Signature
Ensure the integrity of the workbook by adding an invisible digital signature.

Mark as final will make the spreadsheet READ ONLY – no further changes will be accepted. To prevent unauthorized users from opening and viewing the spreadsheet, you need to choose Encrypt with Password. The password you use is case sensitive. You should use a strong password that combines uppercase and lowercase letters, numbers, and symbols. You can have max 255 characters in your password.

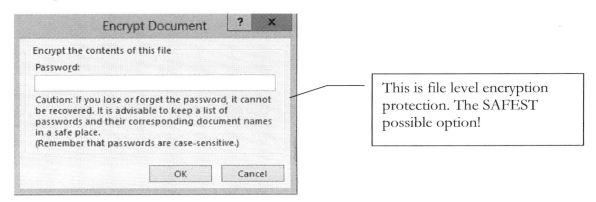

This is file level encryption protection. The SAFEST possible option!

Protect Sheet allows you to select certain specific elements to protect. You primarily do this to prevent a honest user from accidentally or deliberately modifying or deleting important data

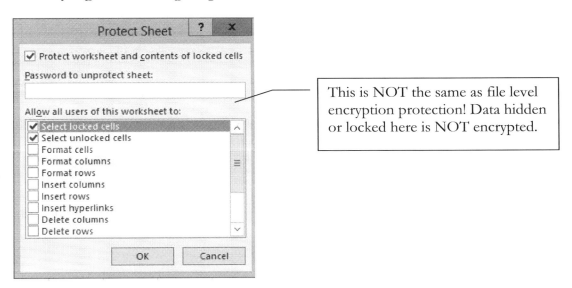

This is NOT the same as file level encryption protection! Data hidden or locked here is NOT encrypted.

If you choose to protect the structure, your worksheets will NOT be allowed to get moved, deleted, hidden, unhidden, or renamed. Also, new worksheets will NOT be allowed to get inserted into the file. When you choose to protect the windows, all the windows will show up at the same size and position as you left them since last time the workbook is opened.

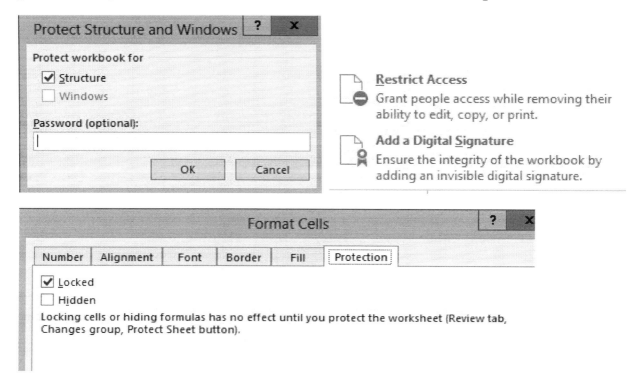

Restrict Access allows you to choose who in the network cannot access your file. To set this up you need to be able to connect to a network server. You may also seal your spreadsheet with a digital certificate, which means you digitally sign it. If you don't already have a digital certificate on your computer, you must first obtain one from somewhere. Excel does not provide you with one. Format Cells- Protection is a protection option at the cell level – you can lock and hide any formulas created in the cells. This option needs to work together with the Protect Sheet function at the REVIEW ribbon (as said in the dialog box). In fact, in the REVIEW ribbon you can also call up the same Protect Sheet / Protect Workbook dialog box.

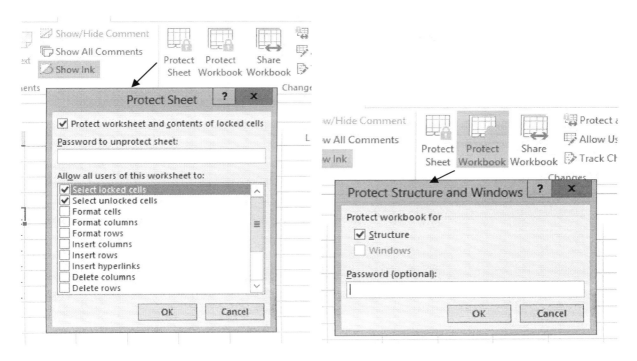

New allows you to create a new file. Open allows you to pick an existing file to open. This file can be local or remote. A remote file is a file shared by another user on another computer. It can be opened only if you have been granted the necessary permissions.

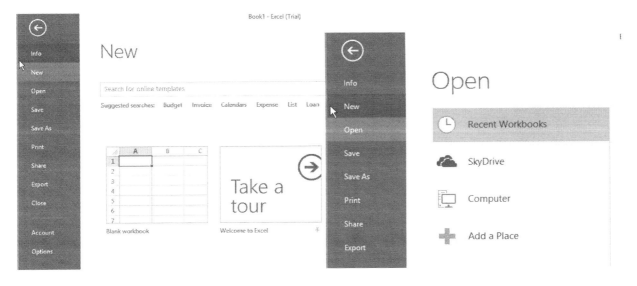

Save is different from Save As. If your file is already named, Save means saving the file without changing the file name and format. Save As gives you the chance to save the file data into a new one or even with a different format. Save As is a function primarily for compatibility – if you need to make the file available to users without Excel 2013, you may need to save the file data using a different format. The default Excel 2013 format is simply "Excel Workbook".

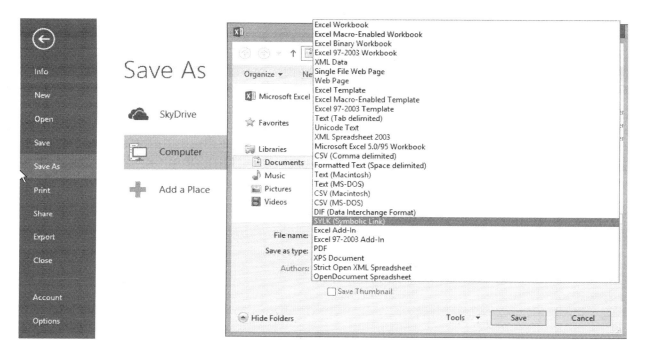

The Print section gives you a range of functions plus a print preview on the right. Printer allows you to pick the printer to use. Printer Properties are printer specific settings that have nothing to do with Excel.

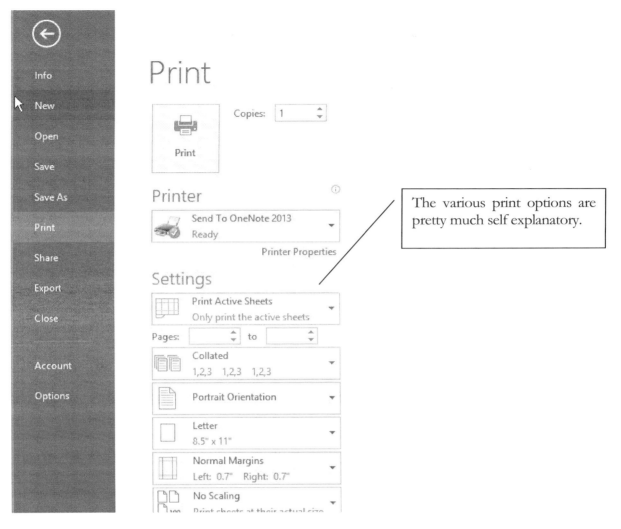

Settings are related to how you want your worksheet to get printed. These are settings that are NOT printer specific. Most functions here are self-explanatory. You may want to use the Collated option if you are printing multiple copies of a multi-page worksheet - this will ensure that your multi-page worksheet is placed in complete sets that you can use immediately.

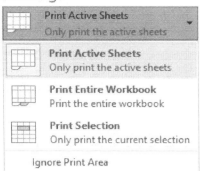 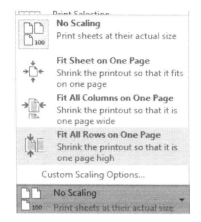

You can also determine the range to print and how they are to get fitted into your paper. The default setting allows you to print the active sheet. If you want to save paper and you don't mind to get smaller print output, you can choose to fit the worksheet into one page and let Excel performs the scaling for you automatically. Page Setup deals with paper size, orientation and margins. You can also set the header and footer here.

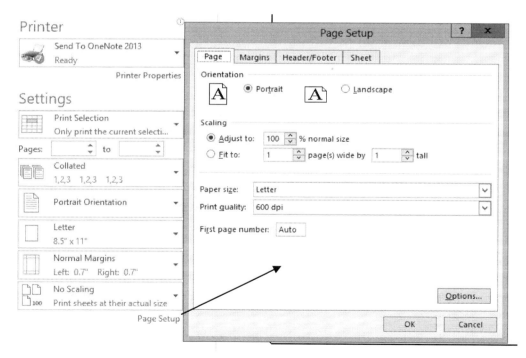

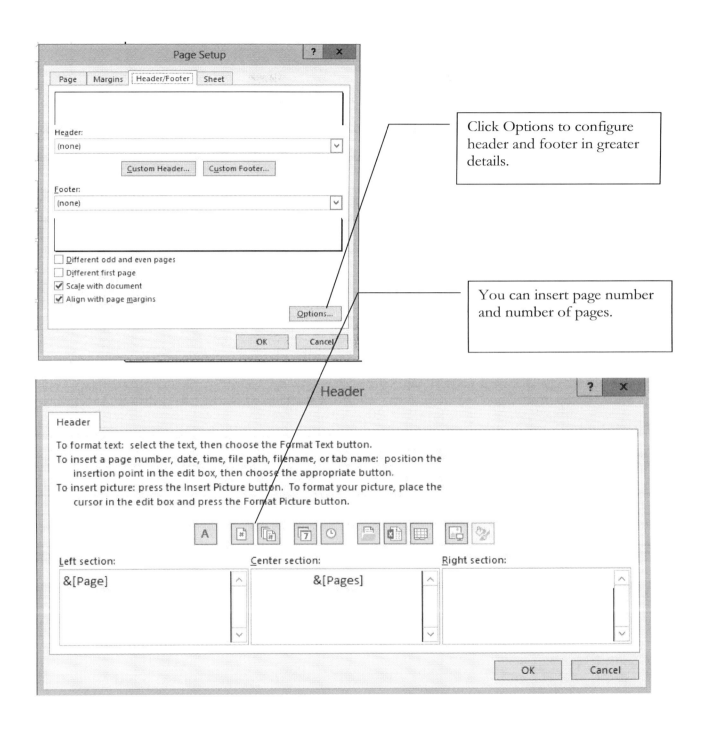

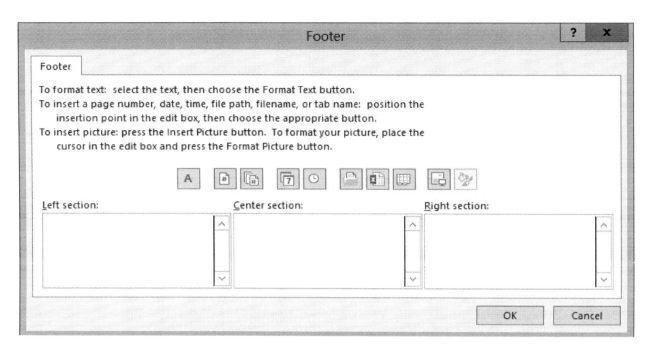

Share allows you to share this file with other people. Export allows you to create PDF and other documents out of it, which is similar to using SAVE AS.

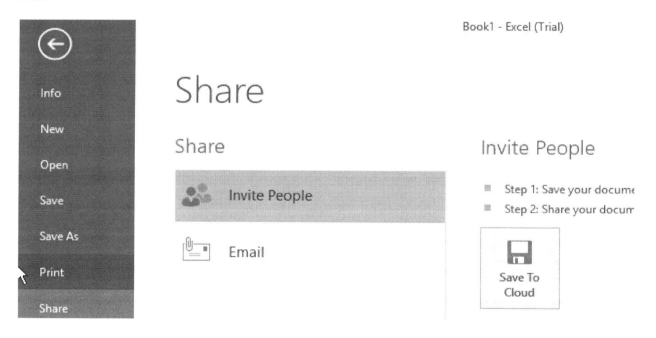

PDF is the way to go if you want to keep the file's format when you share it with other people. PDF file always looks the same on most computers. HOWEVER, Excel cannot read nor edit a PDF file. It can only create one.

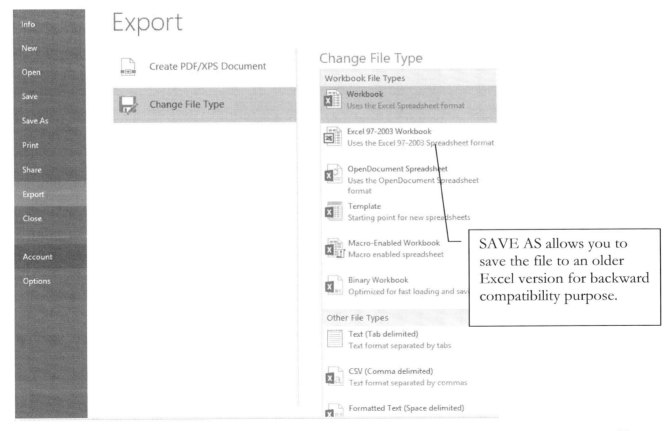

SAVE AS allows you to save the file to an older Excel version for backward compatibility purpose.

Options deals with the Excel program settings, which are not worksheet related at all.

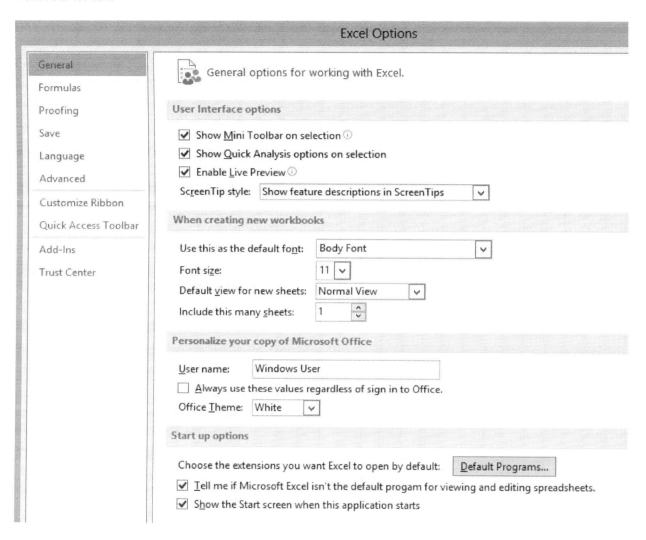

You want to know that in the Trust Center there are options to secure the macros created. The default is Disable all macros with notification, which means macros are disabled but you will get security alerts when there are macros present so you can choose when to enable macros again. Disable all macros except digitally signed macros is similar but macros digitally signed by a trusted publisher can automatically run. Enable all macros means all macros can run without alerts, which can be quite unsafe! Macro will be dealt with in another chapter.

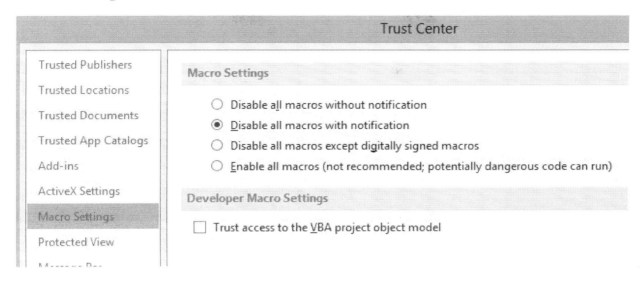

When you edit a worksheet you can always go to HOME – Format – Organize Sheets and either rename or move/copy your worksheets.

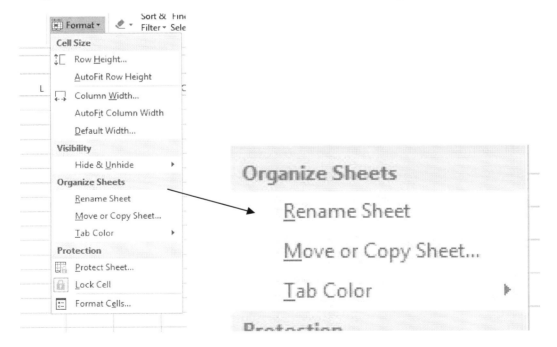

In theory you can have as many worksheets in your workbook as you like.

Copying, Pasting and Filling Cells and Ranges

In a worksheet, a column is the vertical space going up and down the window, identified by a letter. A row, on the other hand, is the horizontal space going across the window, identified by a number. A cell is where the row and column intersect. Each cell has sort of a name assigned according to its column letter and row number.

In a typical spreadsheet you will have three basic types of data, which are label text with no numerical value at all; constants which are fixed numeric values; and formulas. Basic copy and paste is common in all Office software – you either select a cell, a group of cells, or some text inside a cell, then right click and choose Copy/Cut, then move to the target location and choose Paste. OR you can use the Clipboard. You want to know how to use the format painter, which is represented by the little brush like icon.

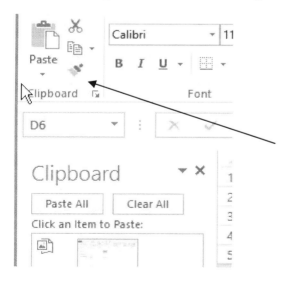

It is for copying the formatting of text. To use it, first select the text that has the formatting to be copied. Then click on it, and then click the text you want to format. Along the process your mouse cursor will be changed to a brush like shape.

Excel is special in that there are many different types of copy and paste operations. For example, Copy as picture allows you to take a snapshot of what you want to copy so that when it is pasted into the target location the same look can be maintained. You often use it to copy and paste cells to another application, such as Word.

Pasting static text is simple. Pasting formulas is not. When you copy a cell that has a equation in it, you need to know what exactly you want to copy – you want to copy the result OR the equation?

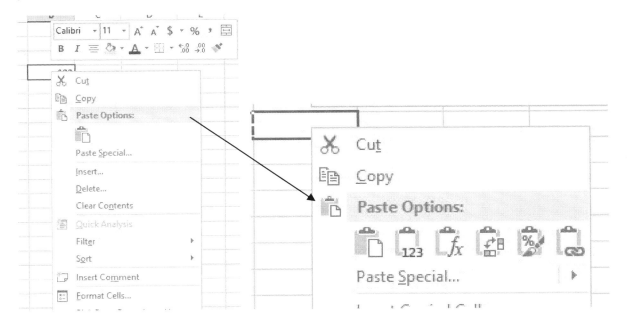

When you right click on the target location, the menu gives you the option of Paste Options. From there you can choose to paste the value, the formula, the formatting, or a combination of all these.

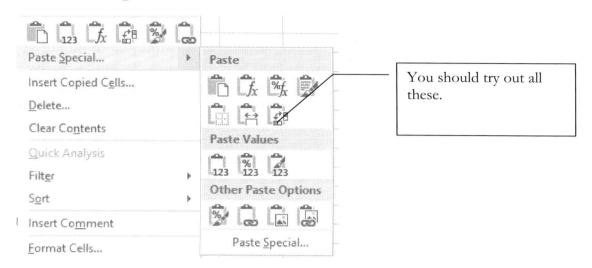

There are so many paste options available but for exam prep purpose you need to pay particular attention to these: Paste All means to paste everything copied. Paste Formulas means to paste all the text, numbers, and formulas copied. Paste Values means only the calculated values. Paste Formats means only to paste the formatting but not the values nor the formulas. Paste Validation means only to paste the data validation rules in the source cell. Paste Formulas and Number Formats means you paste the formulas and also the number formats assigned to the pasted values. Paste Values and Number Formats means you paste the calculated values and also the number formats assigned.

Paste specials gives you some additional options. Skip Blanks means you paste only from the cells that are not blank. Transpose means you change the orientation of the pasted entries along the pasting process. Paste Link establishes a link between the copy and the original entry so that changes made to the original version will also be reflected in the copy.

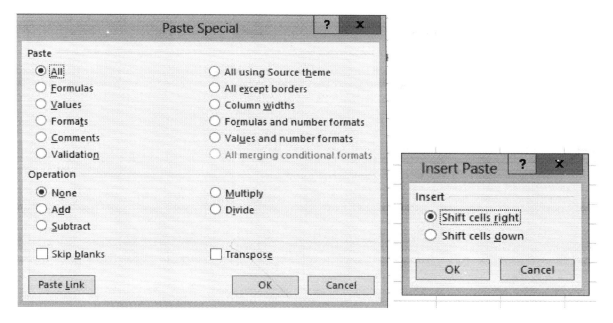

Also note that when you paste something into the target location you need to determine how the existing content in the target location is treated. Normally you can choose to shift it to the right (or down).

You can also merge cells. You need to first select the cells to merge, and then click Merge cells. With Merge and Center, the cell contents will get centered in the merged cell. Do note that those formulas that reference the involved cells will get updated automatically. HOWEVER, you will not be able to sort a range that has both merged and unmerged cells.

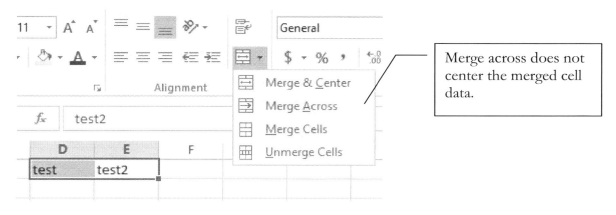

Merge across does not center the merged cell data.

There is also one big problem with cell merging. The screenshot below says it all:

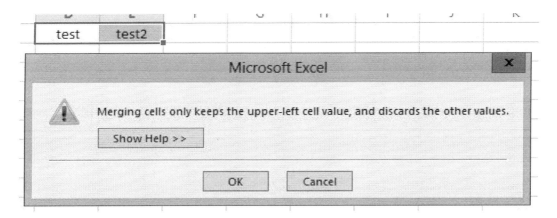

Inserting new cells, rows and columns can be done through Insert. When you insert something you will shift the original cells/rows/columns. Formulas referencing these will be automatically updated unless you have used absolute referencing. We will talk about absolute referencing later in this book.

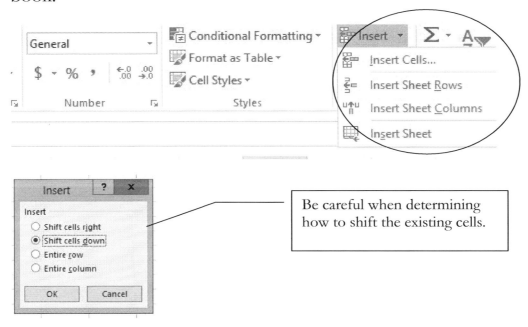

Be careful when determining how to shift the existing cells.

Indenting cells is NOT the same as inserting cells. Indenting is simply about indenting the content within a cell. Indentation is all about setting the distance of the text from the left. You may increase or reduce the indentation as needed.

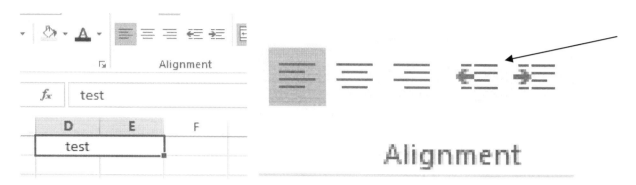

You usually use filling to handle data series. You first select a source cell or a source range of cells, then drag the fill handle (which is on the lower right corner of the source) across or down the cells that you intend to fill. OR, you use the Fill function available on the ribbon to fill:

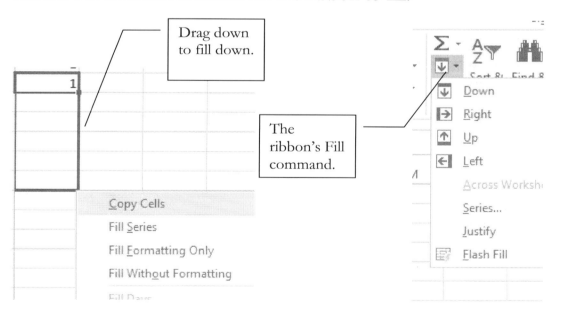

We recommend that you use the right mouse button to drag the fill handle over the range since this will give you a shortcut menu for choosing the appropriate fill operations. If you drag using the left mouse button, the result is a simple auto fill that DOES NOT increment anything on each fill. If you choose Fill Series, each fill is incremented by 1. If you use the Fill function available on the ribbon and choose Series, you can define the step value. A Linear series is calculated by adding the value specified in the Step Value box to each cell, while a Growth series is calculated by multiplying the Step Value by each cell value in turn. On the other hand, if you select Date you can fill with the date incremented automatically.

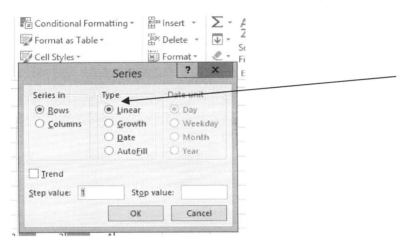

You can click on the Quick Analysis icon which pop up at the lower right of the selected range of cells and select a type of graphical representation to gain a quick preview. You should try out the different options available here.

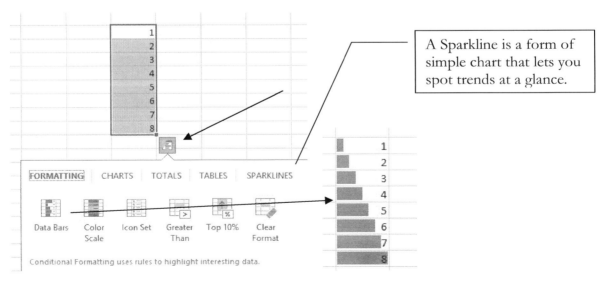

A Sparkline is a form of simple chart that lets you spot trends at a glance.

To clear whatever you have set for a cell or a range of cells, simply choose the Clear command from the ribbon:

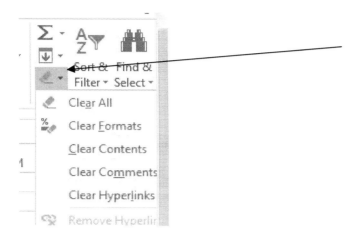

Cell visibility can be configured via HOME – Format. You can choose to hide and unhide rows, columns or even worksheets. Hiding is not the same as deleting – you can unhide an item at any time. And hiding a row or column will not cause any changes to any established equations.

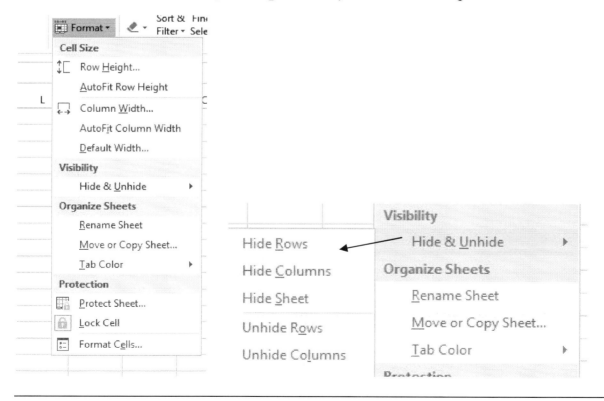

You can perform sorting on cells. First select the cells you want to sort, then click on Sort & Filter from the ribbon:

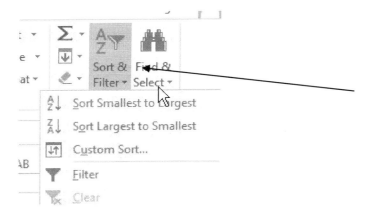

Custom sort allows you to specify multiple sort conditions.

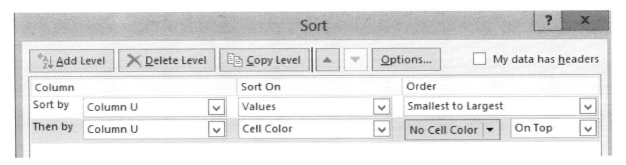

Find & Select allows you to look for and replace certain items from within the worksheet. You will find it useful when your worksheet is large.

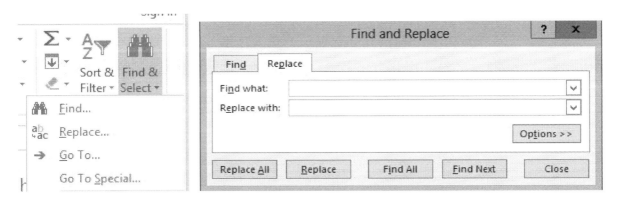

Formatting Cells and Ranges

Whenever you want to change the formatting and style of your cell content, you should select the cell first. After that, from the HOME ribbon you click to open the different formatting dialog boxes. The quickest way is to select a Cell Style:

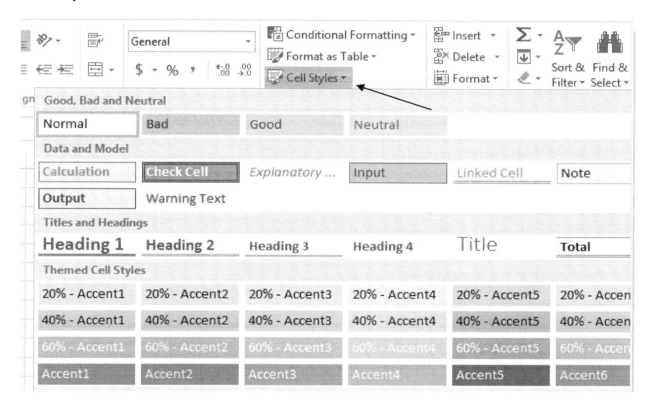

If you want to set just the number format quickly, click on the format pull down menu from the HOME Ribbon:

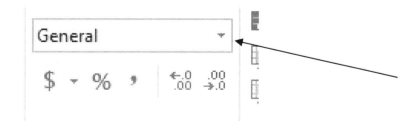

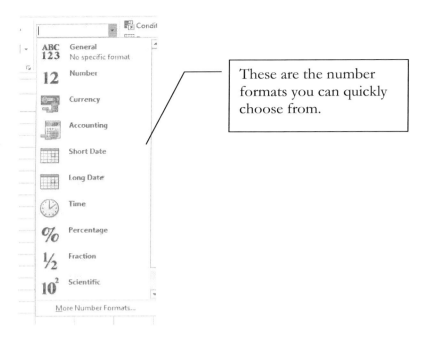

These are the number formats you can quickly choose from.

If you want to also set the text style and other stuff, click to expand Number so the Format Cells dialog box can be called up:

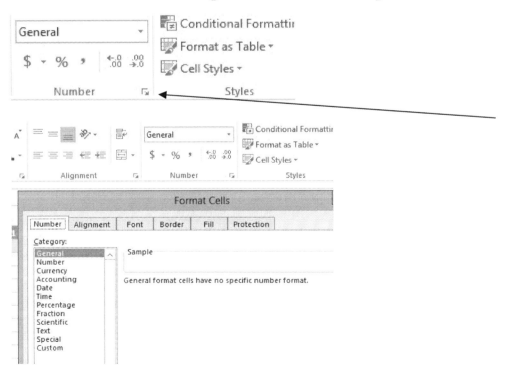

The available number formats are pretty much self explanatory. Number allows you to specify the number of decimal places, the use of thousands separator and how negative numbers should be shown. Currency is for displaying general monetary values. Accounting is for monetary values, just that it will align the currency symbols and any decimal points in a column.

Note that both Number and Currency have a Negative numbers box for selecting the display style for negative numbers.

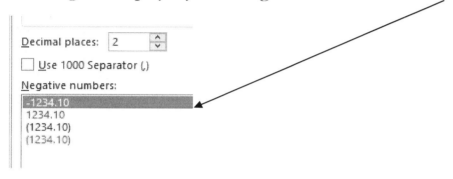

Special is for special formats such as address zip code, phone number and SSN.

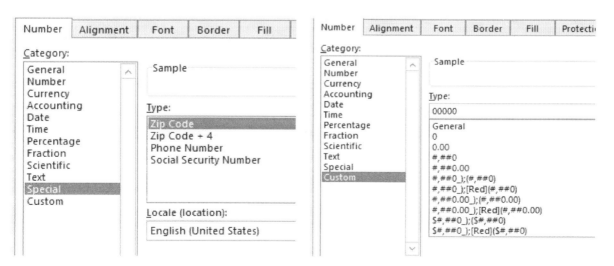

Text shows the cell content as text. In other words, it displays the content as-is. If you want to display both text and number together, you want to create a custom format.

By default, Custom allows you to simply modify a copy of an existing number format code and then save it in the list of number format codes. If you want to display both text and numbers inside one cell, you should enclose the text characters in double quotes " " or precede a single character with a simple backslash \.

Other formatting options are really related to the look and style of the content:

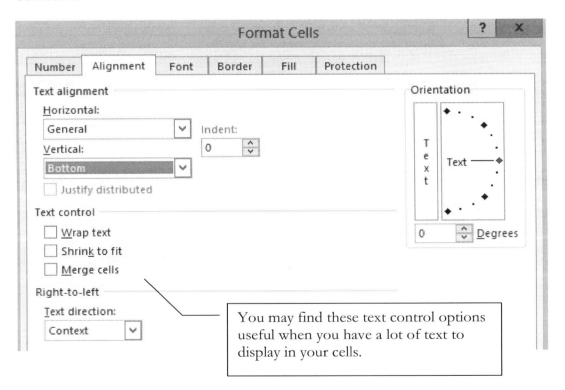

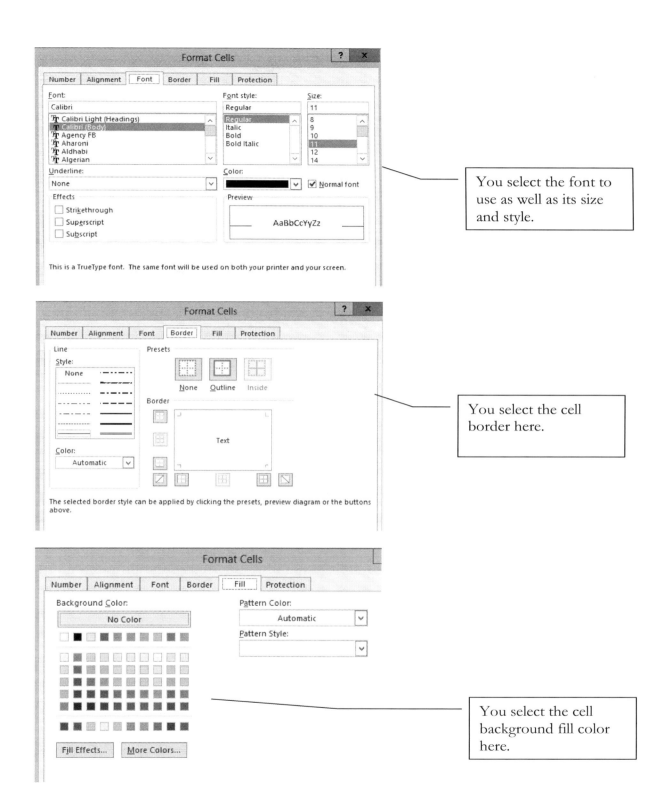

To clear whatever formatting you have set for a cell or a range of cells, simply choose the Clear command from the ribbon and pick Clear Formats:

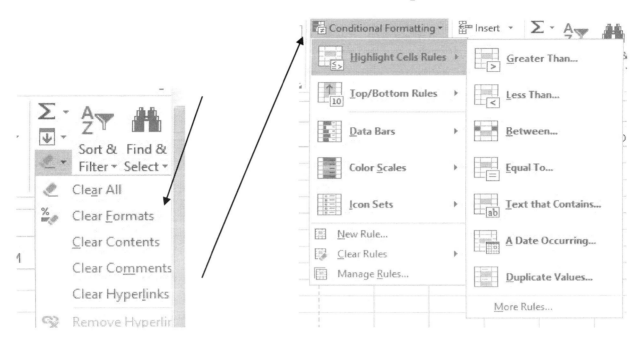

Conditional formatting allows you to control how a cell is formatted when the involved cell data meets the conditions you set for it. A special equation will be set for you so you do not have to manually construct a highly complicated formula by hand.

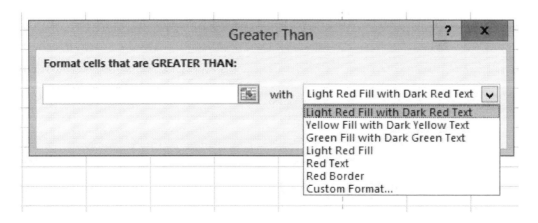

Advanced conditional formatting is covered in the Expert exam.

Lists, Tables and Charts in Excel

You can create a list for purpose of simple data sorting and filtering. First of all the data must be properly laid out. The first row stores the column headings. Each row represents an individual data record. You select all the involved column headings, then right click and choose Filter. Most of the time you will use Filter by Selected Cell's Value.

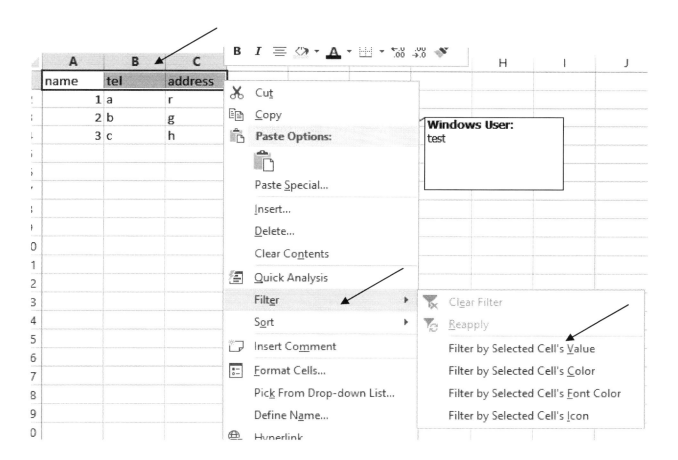

The first column usually acts as the primary record identifier. You click on the down arrow and a list of possible actions will show up.

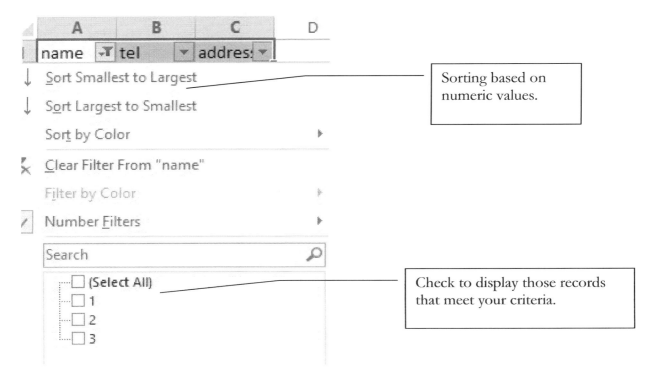

Sorting based on numeric values.

Check to display those records that meet your criteria.

When the column contains numeric values, you will find Number Filters very useful. The available number filters are pretty much self explanatory.

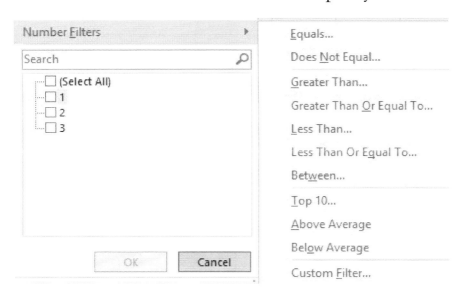

A table allows you to focus your analysis effort in those data include inside the table. "Outside data" is totally excluded. You can either insert a totally new table or format an existing range of cells as table. To create a new table, you need to first select the range of cells that contain the source data, then go to INSERT and choose Table.

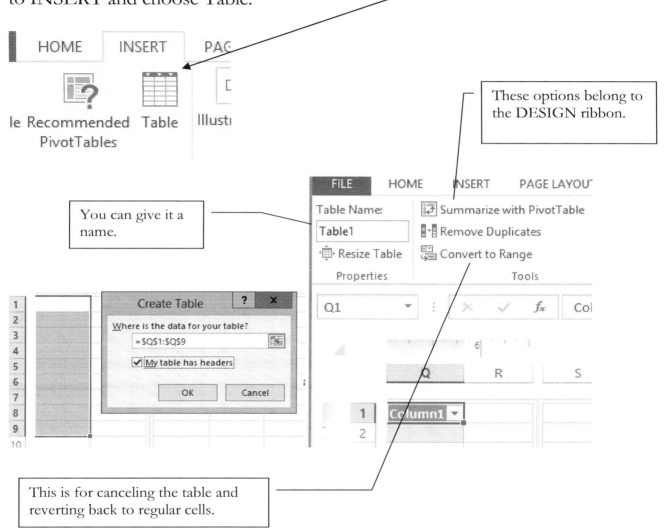

When the table is created successfully, you will see the sort and filter arrows showing up in the row headers. In fact, when you click on the table, you can perform sorting easily.

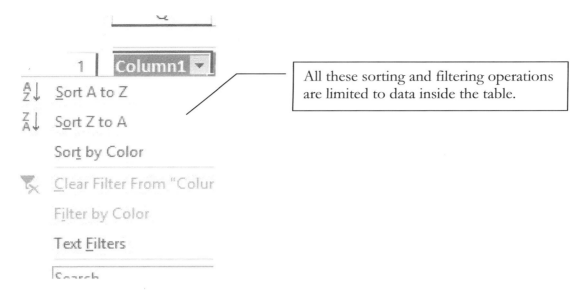

All these sorting and filtering operations are limited to data inside the table.

If you want to quickly format an existing range of cells as a table, first select the cells, then choose HOME – Format as Table.

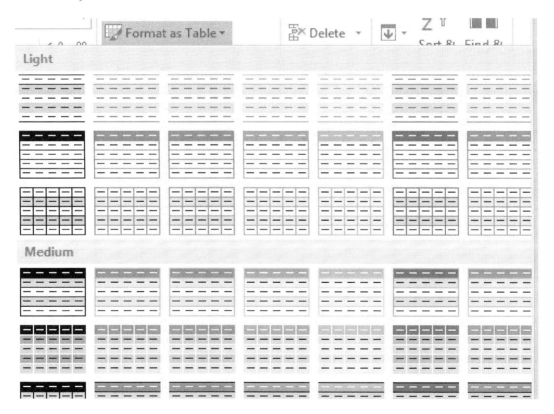

To insert a chart, you need to first select the range of cells that contains the data, then go to INSERT and choose Chart.

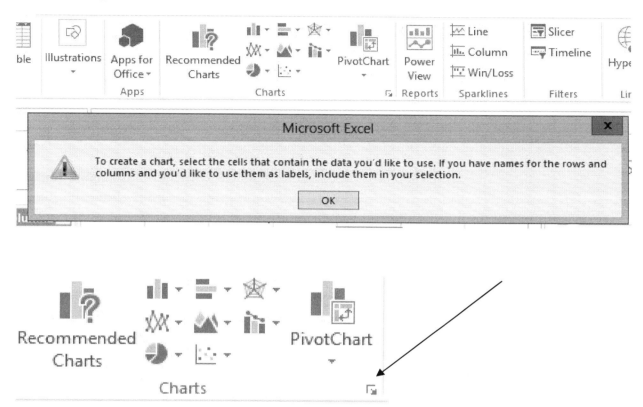

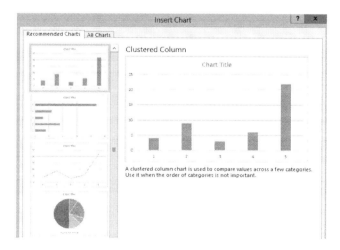

You then select a chart type and have it inserted into the worksheet. The inserted chart will behave just like any other graphical object:

To modify the chart, you will need to use the functions available in the DESIGN ribbon. For example, you can add the necessary chart elements through Add Chart Element, or pick and apply a style through Quick Layout.

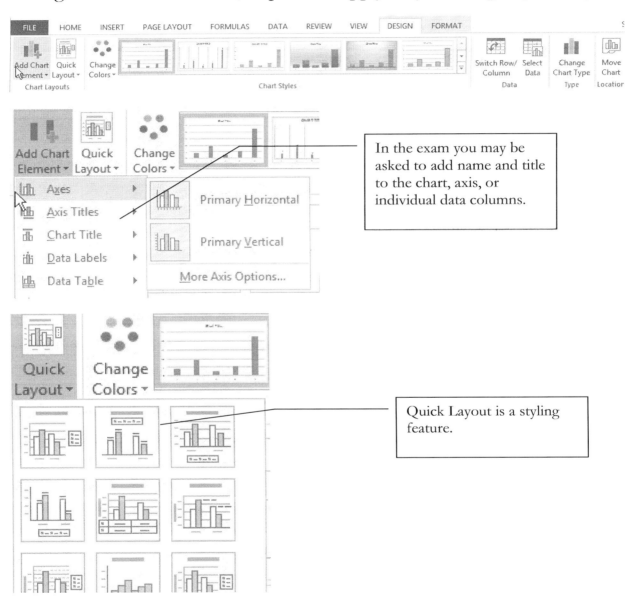

Format Plot Area is for setting the border and background fill color of the chart's plot area, while Select Data Sources allows you to add or edit the data source range.

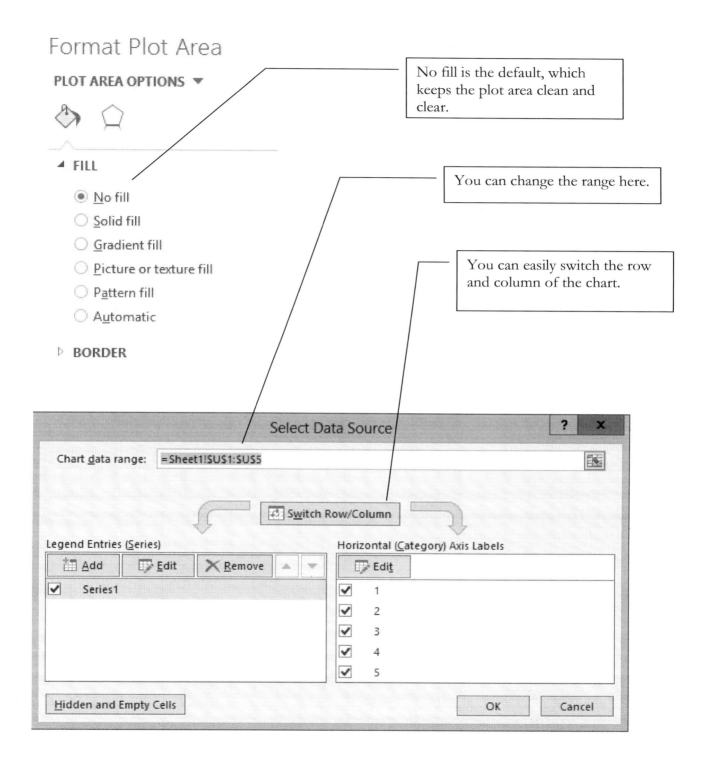

Formulas and Functions

You need to become a little bit more technical here. You need to know how to use references in relative, mixed or absolute form. You also need to know how to reference cell ranges in your formulas. And you must know how to use a number of functions, including:

SUM

MIN and MAX

COUNT

AVERAGE

SUMIF

AVERAGEIF

COUNTIF

RIGHT, LEFT and MID

TRIM

UPPER and LOWER

CONCATENATE

Most functions are available through the HOME ribbon:

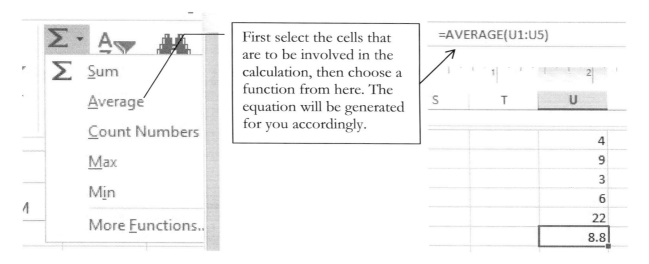

All mathematical equations and functions must start with an equal sign =. There is no exception to this rule. In the equations you will need to make references to other cells. For example: =a1+a2, where a1 and a2 identify the cells being referenced. A1 means column A row 1 while A2 means column A row 2. Basic arithmetic operators you can use include:

Addition - +

Subtraction - -

Multiplication - *

Division - /

When specifying cell references you can either type in the cell references directly or click and drag on the desired cells. To avoid confusion in your exam prep effort we will use the former method. If, say, you want to reference these cells as a range: A1, A2, A3, then you should type A1:A3. If the range includes A1, A2, B1 and B2, then you should type A1:B2. One thing very important about copying and pasting formulas - since cell references information is copied from its relative position, when you paste the equation to another cell the involved cell references will shift accordingly, UNLESS you use absolute positioning when writing the original cell references. That is, instead of writing A1, you write A1. If you write just $A1, then only column A will stay absolute. If you write A$1, then only row 1 will stay absolute. If you write A1 the both will stay absolute, and will not get shifted when pasted to another cell.

With Quick Analysis, Excel can generate simple formulas for you. When you select a range of cells and click on the Quick Analysis icon, choose Totals and you can select from several functions:

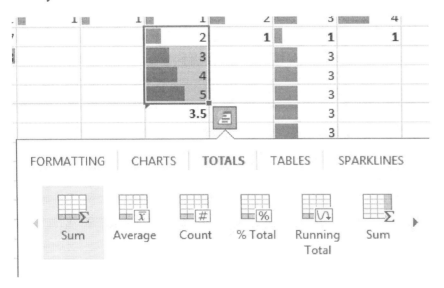

What it does is generating the necessary equations for you. Still, for purpose of exam preparation you should know how to write the equations by hand. Below shows a list of syntaxes for your reference. Remember, NEVER have any blank space in between the "code"!

SUM gives you the total. Example: =SUM(A1:A4)

MIN and MAX retrieve the smallest/largest value out of the selected cells. Examples:

=MIN(A1:A4)

=MAX(A1:A4)

COUNT counts the number of non-empty cells in the entire range of selected cells. Example: =COUNT(A1:A4)

AVERAGE gets you the average value. Example: =AVERAGE(A1:A4)

SUMIF adds logic to the sum operation. See this:

	A	B
1	22	0
2	44	2
3	66	5
4	88	4

If the equation is =SUMIF(B1:B4, ">1", A1:A4), the result is 198. The equation says "if in the range B1 to B4 you find a value larger than 1, then go ahead and include the corresponding value in column A in the SUM operation". In this case we have row 2, 3 and 4 that meet the condition, so we have 44 + 66 + 88 = 198. A1 is omitted since B1 fails to meet the condition of >1. AVERAGEIF and COUNTIF work similarly.

RIGHT, LEFT and MID are for text string manipulation. RIGHT returns the last character in a text string while LEFT returns the first. MID returns a pre-specified number of characters from the text string. See this:

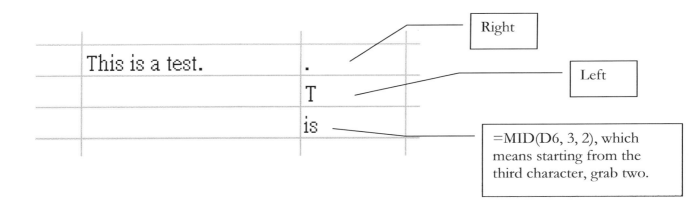

TRIM is for removing all empty spaces from a long text string EXCEPT FOR those regular single spaces between individual words. UPPER and LOWER are for converting to uppercase/lowercase letters. All these functions take a single cell containing the text as their argument. CONCATENATE is different since it can take multiple cells (both number and text are supported) as arguments. You use it to join multiple text strings from different cells for forming one complete string. See this:

=CONCATENATE(B11,C11,D11) ← you cannot use a range as an argument here!

| test1 | test2 | test3 | test1test2test3 |

Textboxes and other Objects in Excel

From the INSERT ribbon you can insert many interesting elements into your worksheet.

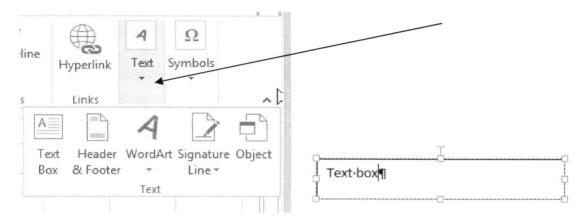

To make a label or comment you can simply insert a text box via Text. The key to using a text box is specifying how it is to be positioned in the worksheet. When you choose to insert a text box, you simply drag it into the worksheet and you may manipulate it freely. If you right click on it, you can change many of its properties:

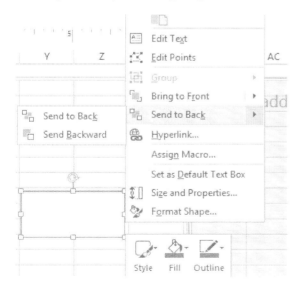

When you have multiple textboxes and shapes in the same place overlapping with one another, you want to fine tune the order they get displayed on screen. To bring anything to the front, choose Bring to Front. To move it up one placement to the front, choose Bring Forward. To send it to the back, choose Send to Back. To send it one placement to the back, choose Send Backward.

WordArt items can be created through Text – WordArt.

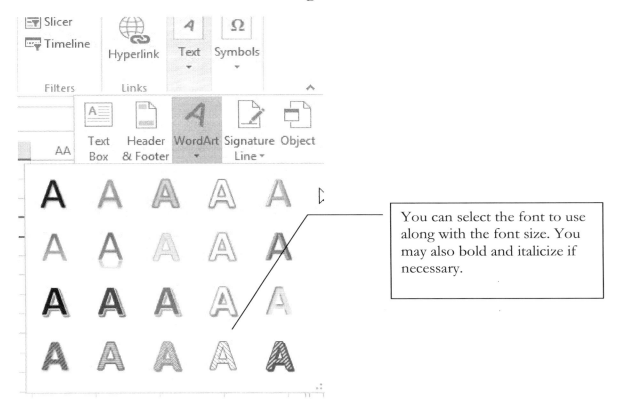

You can select the font to use along with the font size. You may also bold and italicize if necessary.

You can insert a foreign application object into the worksheet via INSERT – Text - Object. You can create a new instance of such foreign object or import from an existing file.

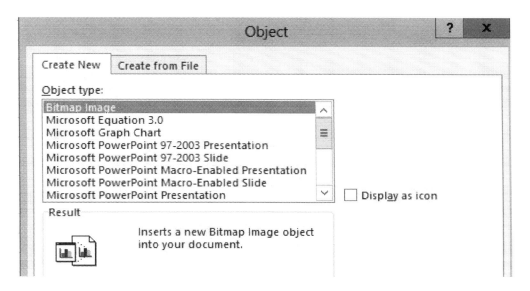

Ready-made shapes can be chosen from INSERT – Illustrations - Shapes.

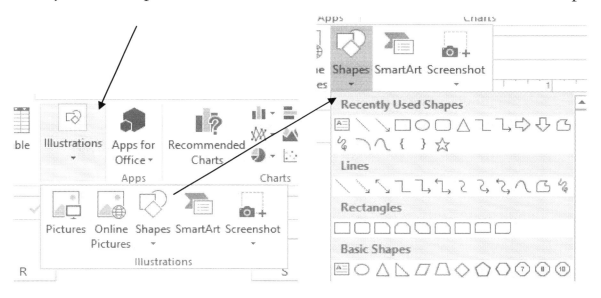

Once a shape is inserted into your worksheet, you can click to select it and make its resize handles visible at each corner and along each edge. You can click and drag on anyone of those to resize the shape. You can also keep the shape's proportions by only dragging the corner handle. You can even squash the shape by dragging a handle along the edge. Note that the green rotation handle at the top can be used to rotate the shape anticlockwise or clockwise.

Bitmap images can be inserted via INSERT – Illustrations - Pictures. Popular image formats like BMP, JPG and GIF are all supported.

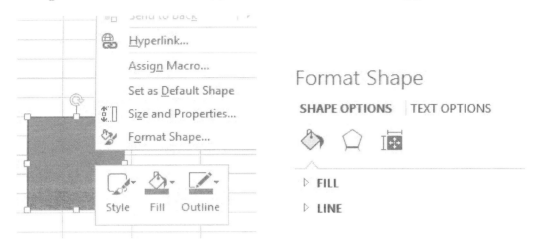

You can always right click on an object to access its menu. Format Shape allows you to set color fill, line style and other special effects such as shadow, glow and reflection. It calls up the Format Shape dialog box, which has both text options and shape options available. You can also change the shape to a textbox via the text options.

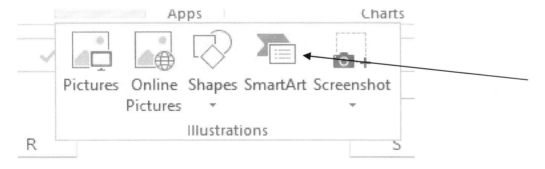

A SmartArt graphic is a fancy visual representation of textual information. You can easily input static text into a SmartArt graphic. All you need to do is to click on the SmartArt icon, then choose from the available designs and insert your choice into the worksheet.

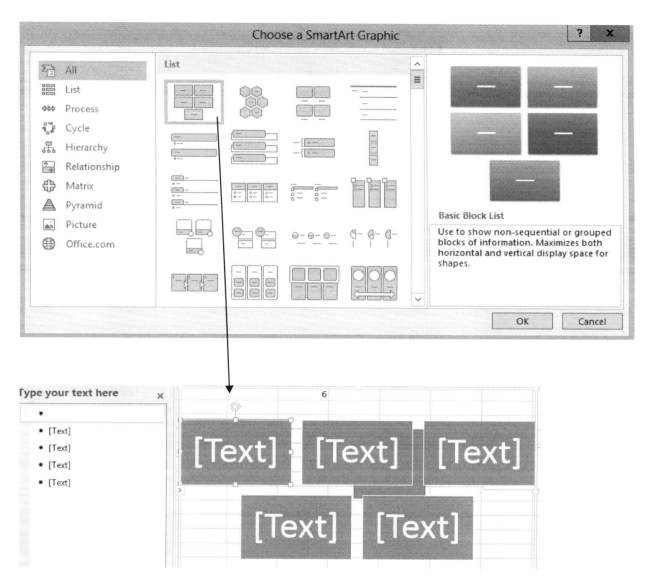

Once the graphic is inserted into the worksheet, you can click on it to key in your textual content. You can in fact change and edit the individual shapes that form the SmartArt graphic. Or you can add new shapes into it. Just right click on the SmartArt graphic and you will see the corresponding menu options.

Unlike textboxes, comments are not visible for printing. You can right click on a cell and click Insert Comment. Later on you can right click again to Edit Comment.

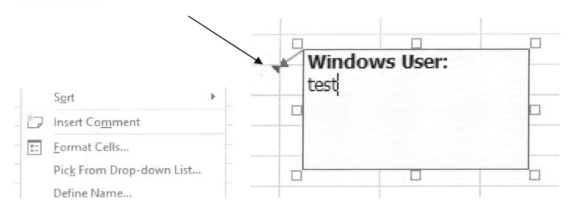

Normally the comment box would not show up unless you place the mouse cursor over the little red triangle on the upper right corner of the cell. If you want to show all comments altogether, simply choose REVIEW – Show All Comments.

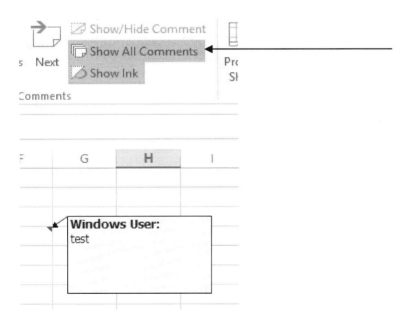

Macro and Shortcut Keys in Excel

Macros is an automation feature for automating your frequently performed tasks. A macro records what you have done and replays your actions. On the right-most part of the VIEW ribbon you can find Macros. Click on it and choose Record Macro to record a new one.

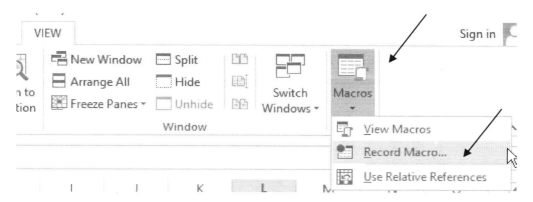

You may want to assign the macro to, say, a shortcut key combination so you can easily call it up. The key combination has to include the Ctrl key though. Also, by default this macro stays with the current workbook only, which is good enough for purpose of the exam.

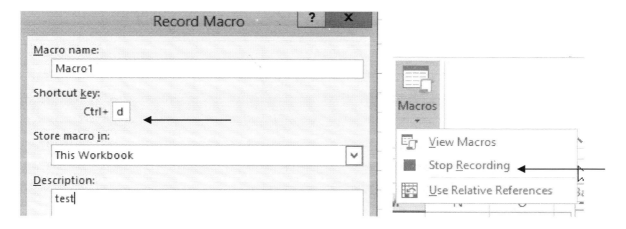

When you finish your actions, simply click Macros again and choose Stop Recording. Now the macro is saved in the list of macros. You can either use the short cut key combination to run it, or simply select it and click Run. To run a recorded macro, click Macros – View Macros and choose from the list accordingly.

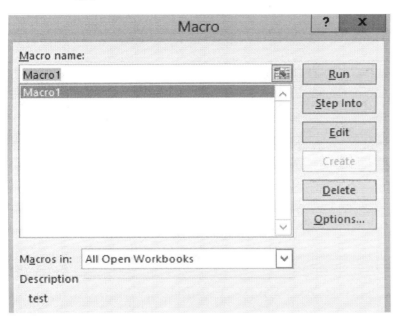

If you click Edit you will go into the VBA (Visual Basic for Application) coding mode, which is way beyond the scope of regular spreadsheet usage. Since macro can be coded, it is possible for a destructive macro to spread like a virus. Macro security is something to be configured in the Trust Center we mentioned earlier in this book.

The Outlook Environment and Settings

Below shows the screen you will see when you first start up Outlook.

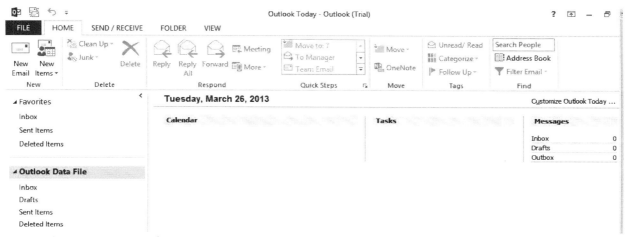

Usually you would want to first configure the email account settings (you should have been provided with all the necessary account settings before you do this). Server side configuration information is NOT your responsibility. You click FILE and then click Add Account to call up the Add Account window.

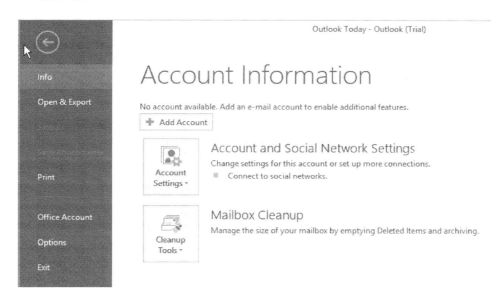

Outlook is supposed to use a process known as Autodiscover to automatically detect your account/server side settings based on the name and password you entered, assuming you have a working network with Exchange server in place. Manual configuration is primarily for setting connection with your ISP server.

Add Account

Auto Account Setup
Outlook can automatically configure many email accounts.

⦿ **E-mail Account**

Your Name: mike
Example: Ellen Adams

E-mail Address: mike@examreview.net
Example: ellen@contoso.com

Password: ********
Retype Password: ********
Type the password your Internet service provider has given you.

○ **Manual setup or additional server types**

Add Account

Choose Service

⦿ **Microsoft Exchange Server or compatible service**
Connect to an Exchange account to access email, calendars, contacts, tasks, and voice mail

○ **Outlook.com or Exchange ActiveSync compatible service**
Connect to a service such as Outlook.com to access email, calendars, contacts, and tasks

○ **POP or IMAP**
Connect to a POP or IMAP email account

You need to use this if you are connecting to the outside ISP.

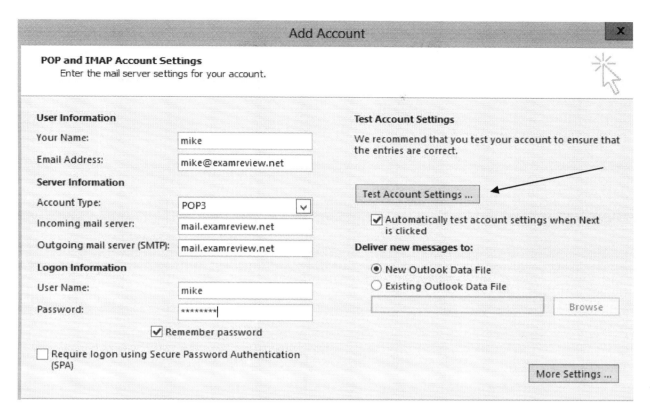

You can click on the Test Account Settings button to generate and send test email to your email account. Make sure your username and password have been entered correctly! Do note that this testing process can be made optional, although testing is always recommended.

An Outlook data file is a Personal Folders file in .pst format that saves your data locally. If you are using an Exchange Server account, your data will be saved on the mail server but with an Offline Folder file located on your computer in case you need to work without a working connection. Just remember, when you run Outlook for the first time all the necessary data files will be created automatically so you may not need to create any new file explicitly. Also, if you are using an Exchange Server account you should not need any local Outlook data file.

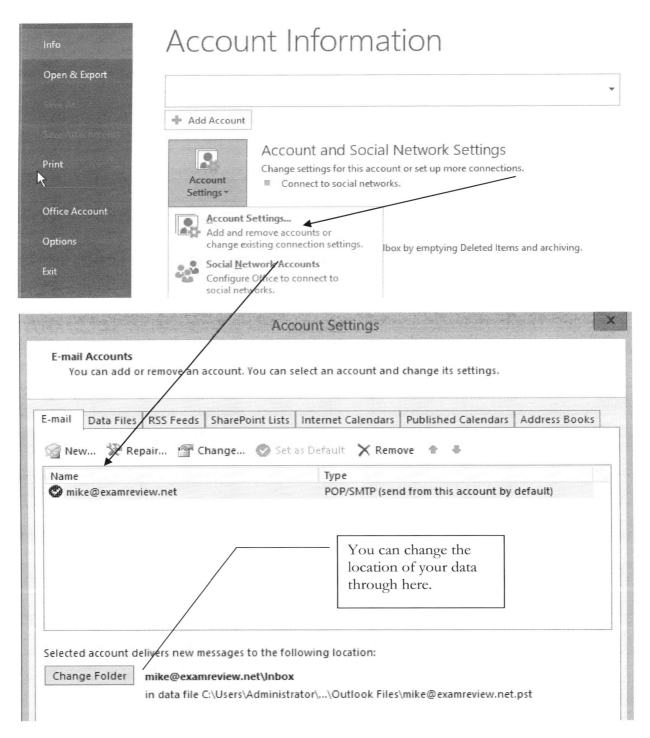

Account Settings allows you to modify the existing account settings. You can also check and verify the status of the existing accounts through here.

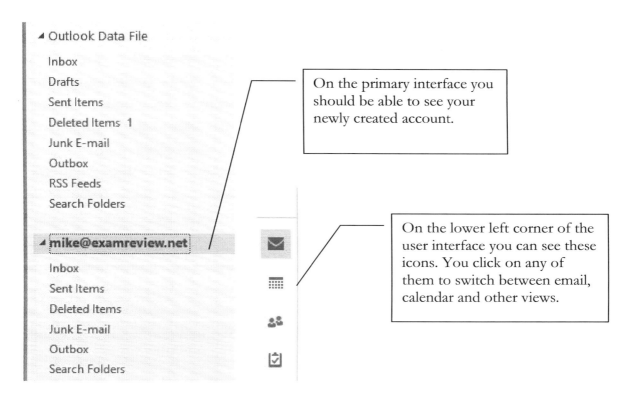

Additionally you may configure your account to join a social network such as Facebook. You do so via Account Settings – Social Network Accounts.

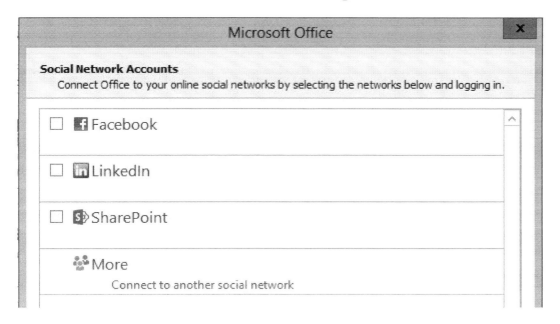

To properly manage the mailbox size you want to perform regular mailbox cleanup. Through Cleanup Tools - Mailbox Cleanup you can check the size of your mailbox and folders, find out oversized items and clean them up accordingly. Empty Deleted Items Folder is for an irreversible deletion of items for true space saving. Archive is all about moving older items you still want to keep to a separate .pst file that you can open again later in the future. Doing so can reduce the size of your current .pst file and speed things up.

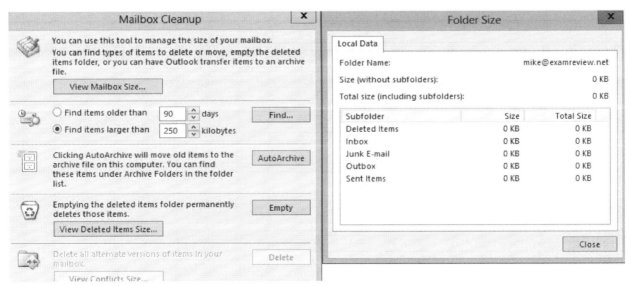

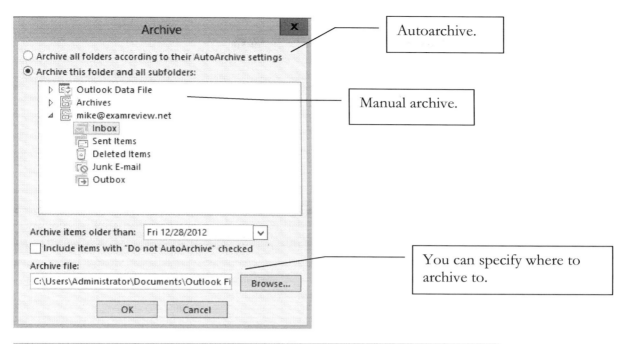

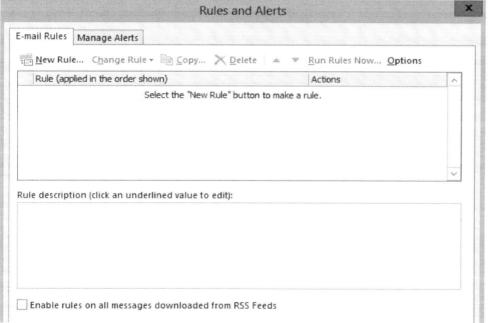

A rule instructs Outlook to act automatically upon incoming or outgoing messages based on pre-specified conditions. You can click on New Rule… to invoke the Rules Wizard. Note that if you use an Exchange Server account, some rules are server-based rules that run on the server side. Client-only rules, on the other hand, are rules that run locally on your computer without any server involvement.

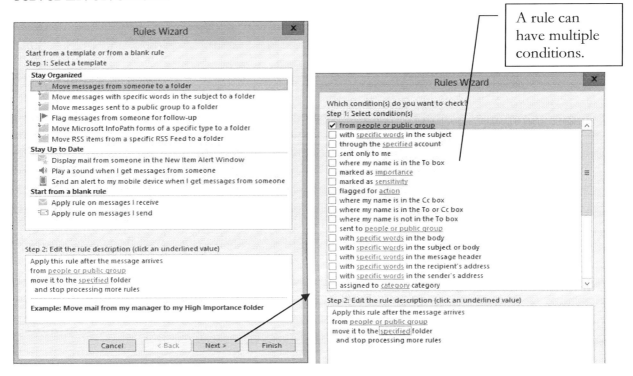

Alerts is not the same as rules. It is simply a feature that helps you stay updated when items on your site change. You click Manage Alerts – New Alert… to create new alerts.

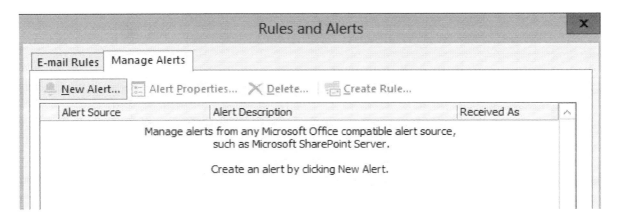

Print allows you to configure basic printer settings. Unlike Word and Excel, there are too many options for you to configure here.

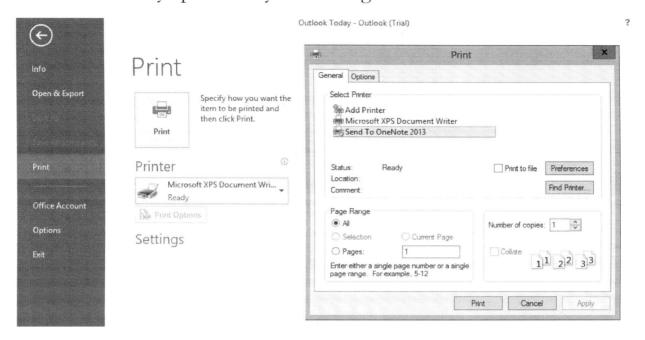

Options - Outlook Options allows you to configure program-wide settings.

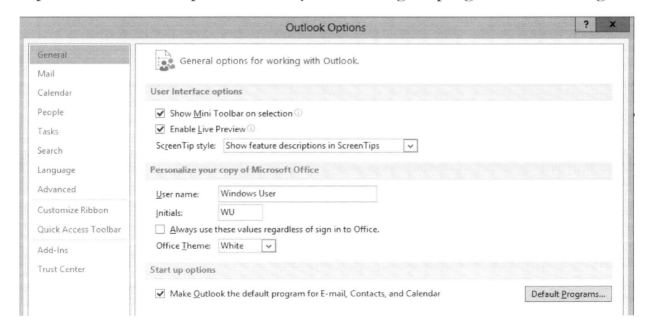

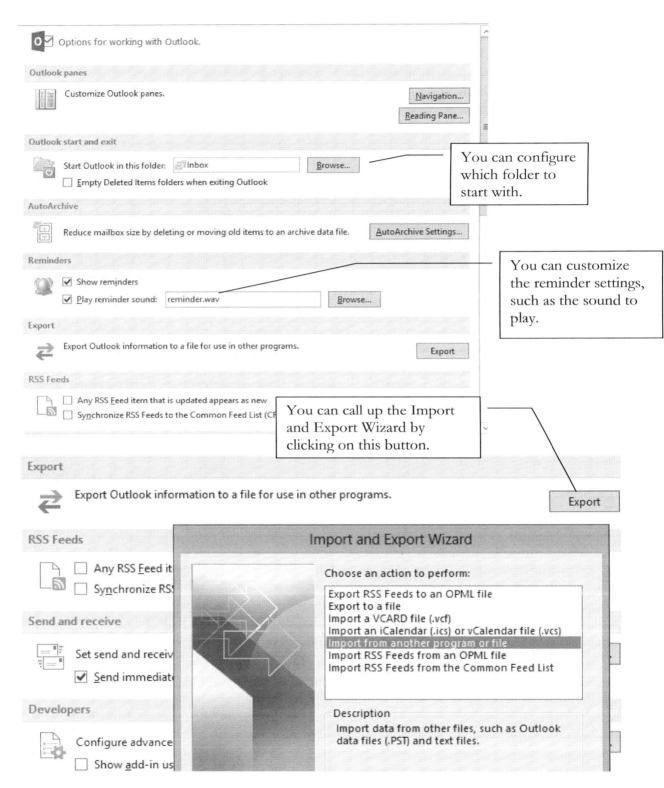

Trust Center deals with security. You click on the Trust Center Settings button to reach the Trust Center dialogs.

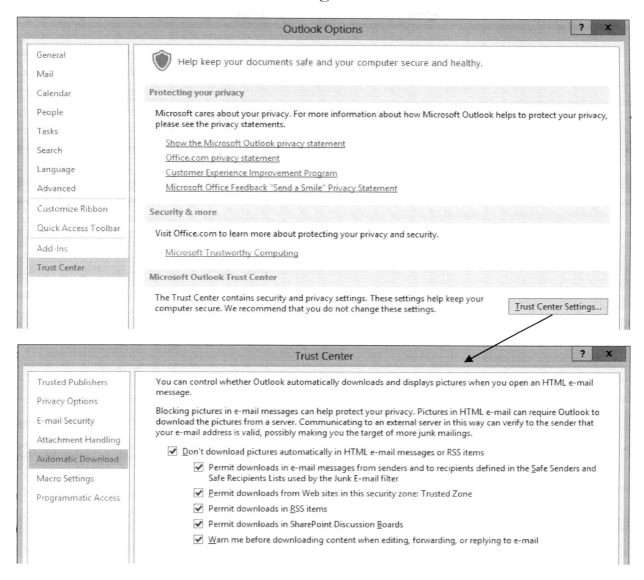

You need to pay attention to Automatic Download, Attachment Handling and Email Security. HTML based email messages may include pictures or sounds that are to be downloaded separately when the message is previewed. This can become problematic when junk email senders make use of so called web beacons for spamming. The default setting is to NOT automatically download pictures and other content UNLESS you explicitly decide to view the content. When automatic picture downloads is blocked, areas that should have a picture shown will be displayed with a red X. The recommended practice is for you to download pictures on a per email basis - you can display a picture simply by right clicking it.

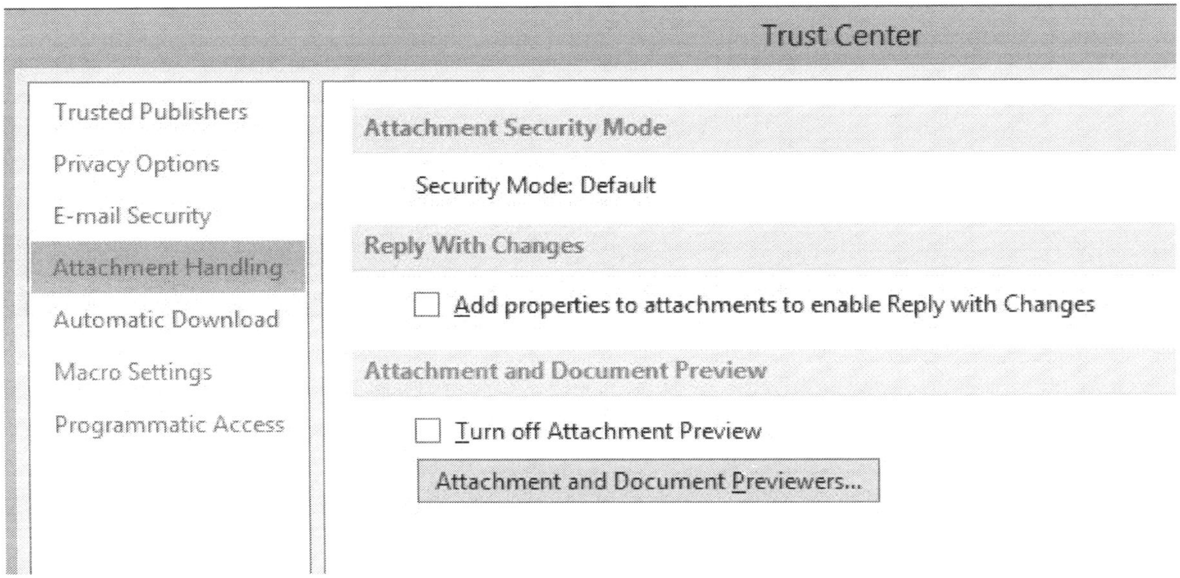

```
Trust Center
─────────────────────────────────────────────
Trusted Publishers      Attachment Security Mode
Privacy Options             Security Mode: Default
E-mail Security         Reply With Changes
Attachment Handling         ☐ Add properties to attachments to enable Reply with Changes
Automatic Download
Macro Settings          Attachment and Document Preview
Programmatic Access         ☐ Turn off Attachment Preview
                            [ Attachment and Document Previewers... ]
```

By default, the Attachment Security Mode is set to block all executable files. Although it is possible to unblock executable files by changing the Attachment Security Mode, you shouldn't do this for the sake of security. Attachment preview allows you to see a preview of the message attachments instead of opening each attachment manually. You should realize that even having a preview can be unsafe, and that's why its default is set to off.

Email encryption and digital signatures are the options available in Email Security. Outlook itself does not come with any digital certificate or digital ID so you must obtain them from the network administrator in order to get them to work.

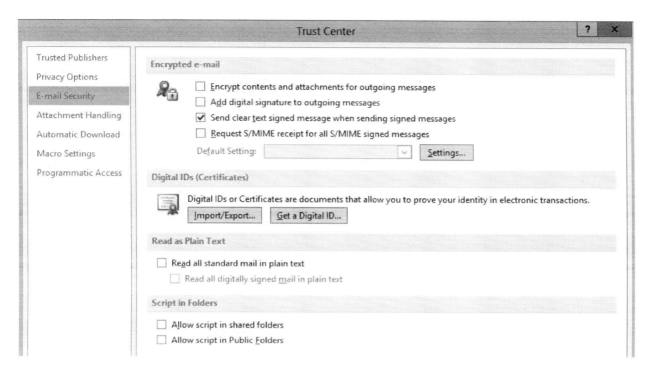

If you choose Add digital signature to outgoing messages, ALL outgoing messages will be automatically signed. This may produce problems if the recipient does not have a capable email reader. To be safe, also enable Send clear text signed message when sending signed messages. This way everyone can read your messages for sure.

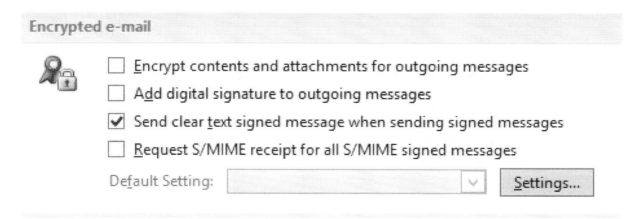

OR, you can add digital signature on a per message basis via Options – Tracking – Security Settings.

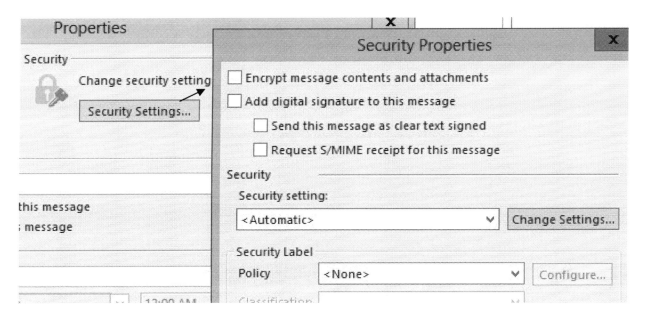

To select a certificate for use with this message, further click Change Settings…

Privacy Options allow you to configure Outlook to perform language transaction using online dictionary. You can select from the list of available language pairs.

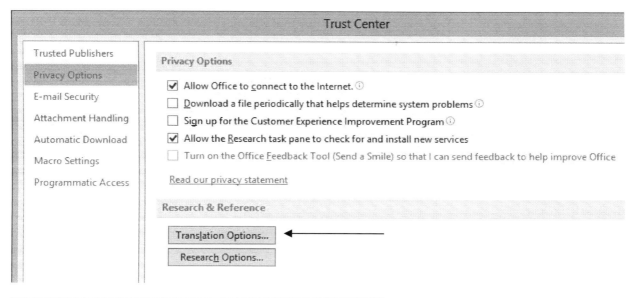

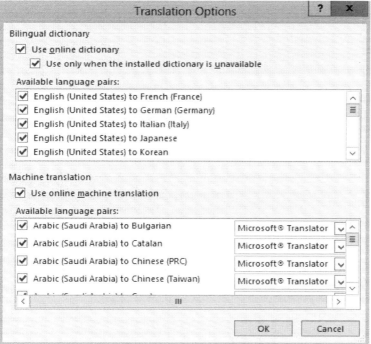

Research options refer to the specific reference books and sites that are to be used for providing research services such as dictionaries, thesauruses ...etc.

Outlook Today is a feature which provides a quick snapshot of your calendar, tasks, meetings and mail for today. On the right side you can click Customize Outlook Today to call up the Customize Outlook Today window. The options available are pretty much self explanatory. If you don't want to see it, simply uncheck the option at the startup section.

You can also click Choose Folders to pick the mail folder(s) to be displayed.

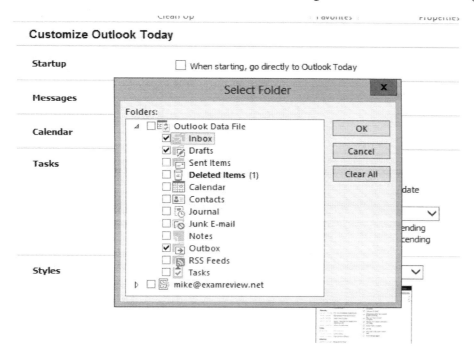

REVIEW provides services such as spelling/grammar check, word count and thesaurus …etc.

VIEW – View Settings allows you to customize the view settings. A view is simply the layout that displays your Outlook items.

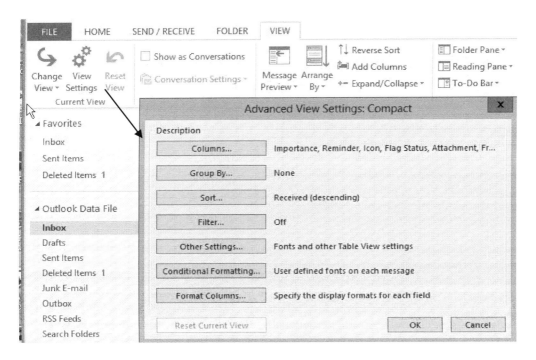

By default the filter is off. You can click Filter ... to control what messages are displayed and what are not, or click Sort... to arrange the messages display order.

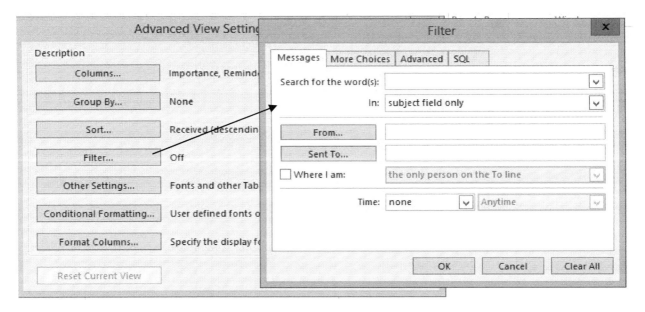

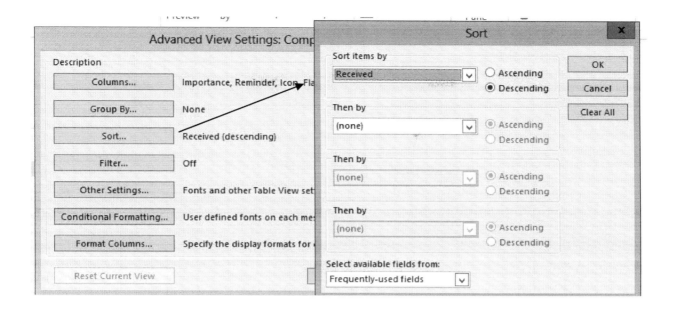

Conditional Formatting… allows the view to display certain messages in specific format based on different conditions.

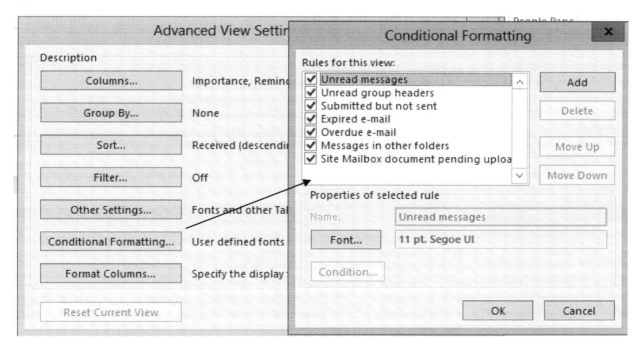

Outlook Email Formatting

There are several similarities between email and regular snail mail. Both need to have a unique address. And both need to be "sent" and "picked up". The difference is that with email everything takes place electronically. Email addresses are unique. The domain part of the addresses actually determines what post office the mail will be sent to for delivery. Email has a unique post office, which is the email server. Each email server has a unique name. When you send your email the last part of the address after the @ is the server address. You do need several things to send and receive email. You need a working Internet connection, an email account, and also an email software package (in this case, we have Outlook).

In Outlook, email sending and receiving are all done through the HOME ribbon. To send new emails, you either click on New Email or New Items – Email Message.

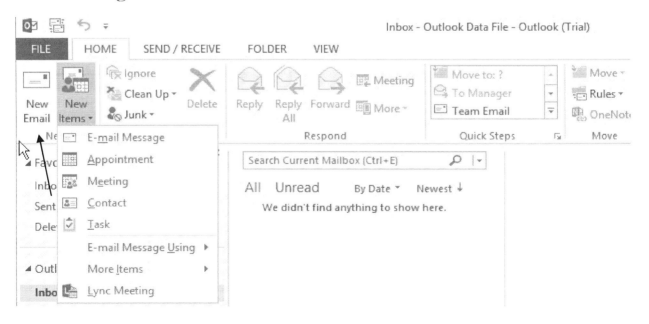

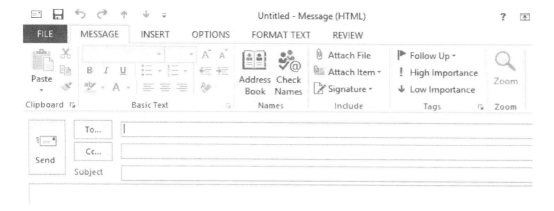

If you click TO you can open up your contact list and search for your recipient. You can send to multiple recipients.

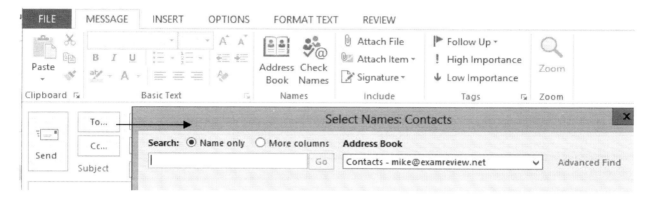

When everything is ready (the subject and the message content), you can hit the Send button to send the email.

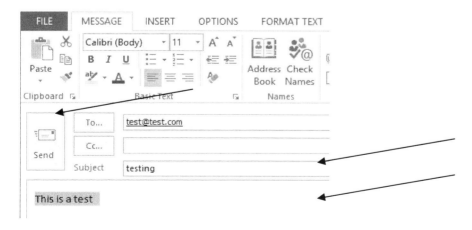

One thing you want to know about Outlook email messages is that you can actually edit the message text just like what you do in MS Word. You can change the font, set the colors and style, set indentation and lists, and change paragraph settings. If you have experience with Word you will have no problem here at all.

Themes (available on the OPTIONS ribbon) are like templates – they have preset styles on every element of the message body (color, text, background, layout …etc.). To be precise, a theme is a collection of formatting choices you can apply to an entire message. A style is a predefined combination of formatting choices specifically for fonts that can be applied to certain selected text but not to the entire message.

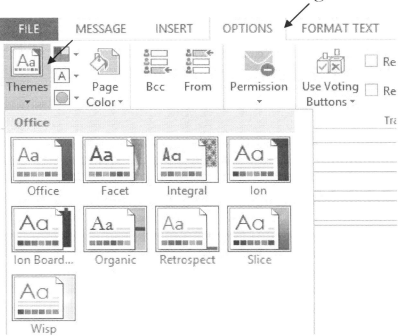

Whenever you want to change the formatting style of some of your text, you should select the desired text first. After that, from the FORMAT TEXT ribbon you click to open the different formatting dialog boxes. All the font related options are pretty much self-explanatory.

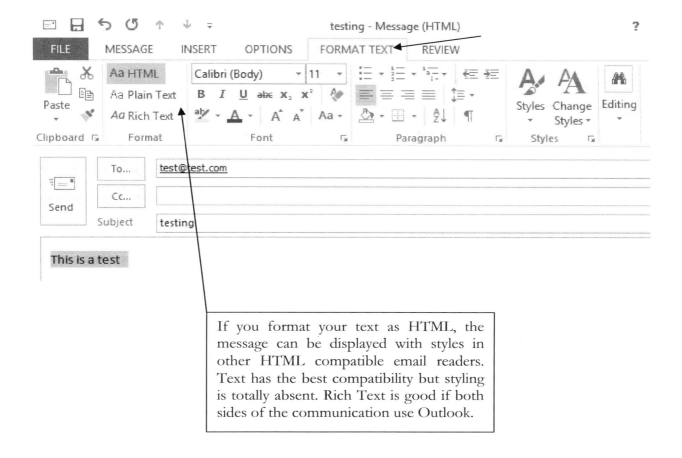

If you format your text as HTML, the message can be displayed with styles in other HTML compatible email readers. Text has the best compatibility but styling is totally absent. Rich Text is good if both sides of the communication use Outlook.

On the other hand, if you simply want to change text alignment (the default is left), use this toolbar:

A list can be bulleted or numbered. On the FORMAT TEXT ribbon you can find a tab that shows the lists. First highlight the pieces of text that are supposed to form your list, then click the List tab and choose a list format.

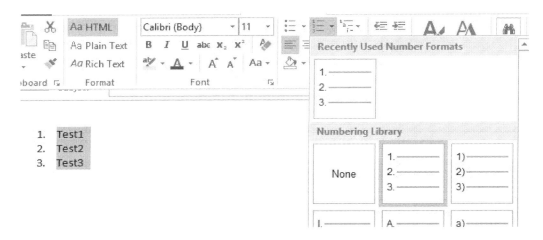

Paste Options (available when you right click) allows you to paste while retaining the source formatting, paste only as text with nothing else, or paste while following the destination formatting.

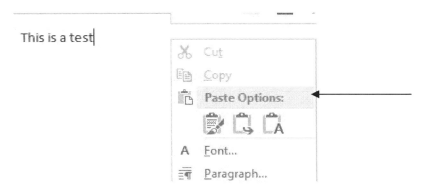

The INSERT ribbon allows you to insert extra objects into the message.

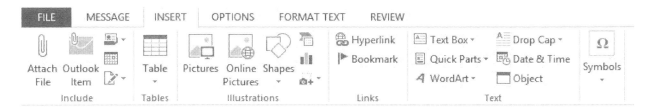

Tables are for laying out text and/or graphics. You can set borders and shading for them, or you can keep them transparent. You use the INSERT ribbon to insert a new table – from the menu you can quickly "draw" a new table by dragging over the cells.

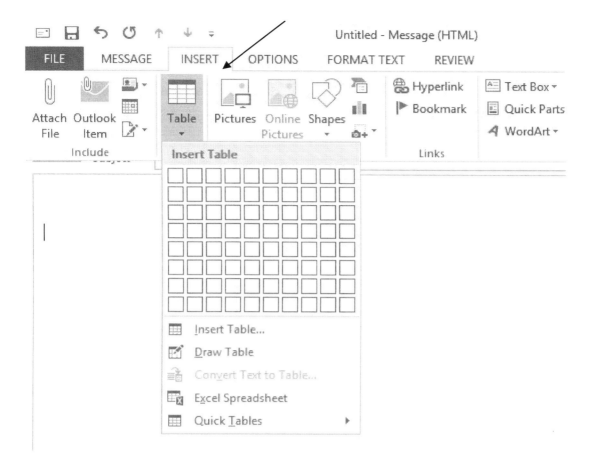

To change the formatting of an existing table, click on the upper left corner to select the entire table, and you will see a popup menu. From there you can choose to set the border and shading. You can also directly drag on the table column/row/cell to change their size.

You can insert a text box into the message. The key to using a text box is specifying how it is to be positioned. When you choose to insert a text box, you simply drag it into the message body and you may manipulate it freely.

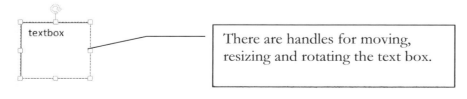

There are handles for moving, resizing and rotating the text box.

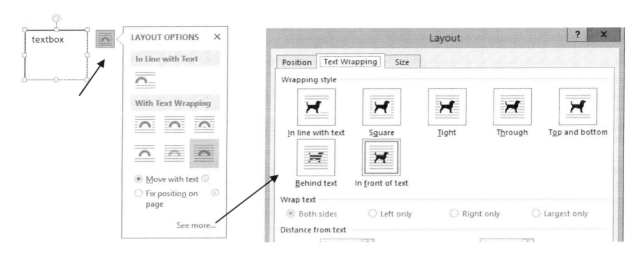

If you right click on it, you can actually change the wrap text settings. Keep in mind, these wrap text settings are available for text boxes and also for all other objects such as drawings, shapes, WordArts …etc. The best way to learn how these settings differ is for you to try them out yourself!

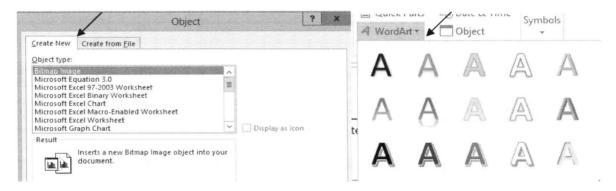

You can insert a foreign application object via INSERT – Object. You can create a new instance of such foreign object or import from an existing file. Ready-made shapes can be chosen from INSERT – Shapes. WordArt items can be created through INSERT – Insert WordArt.

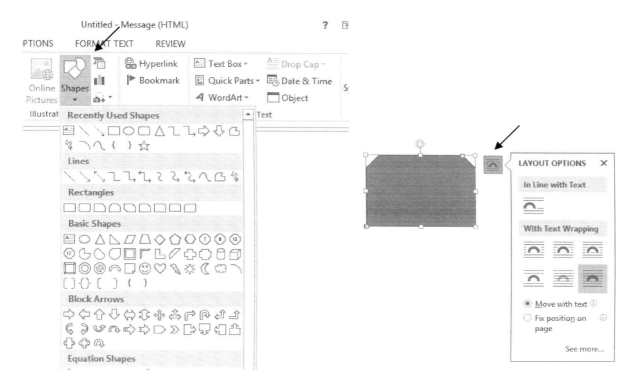

Once a shape is inserted into your document, you can click to select it and make its resize handles visible at each corner and along each edge. You can click and drag on anyone of those to resize the shape. You can also keep the shape's proportions by only dragging the corner handle. You can even squash the shape by dragging a handle along the edge. Note that the green rotation handle at the top can be used to rotate the shape anticlockwise or clockwise.

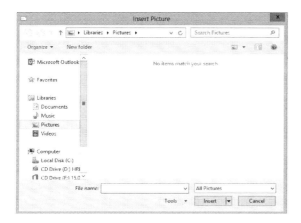

Bitmap images can be inserted via INSERT – Pictures. Popular image formats like BMP, JPG and GIF are all supported. Once an object is placed inside a document, you can always right click on it to access its menu. More Layout Options allows you to precisely set the object's position and layout by keying in numerical measurements. Format Shape allows you to set color fill, line style and other special effects such as shadow, glow and reflection.

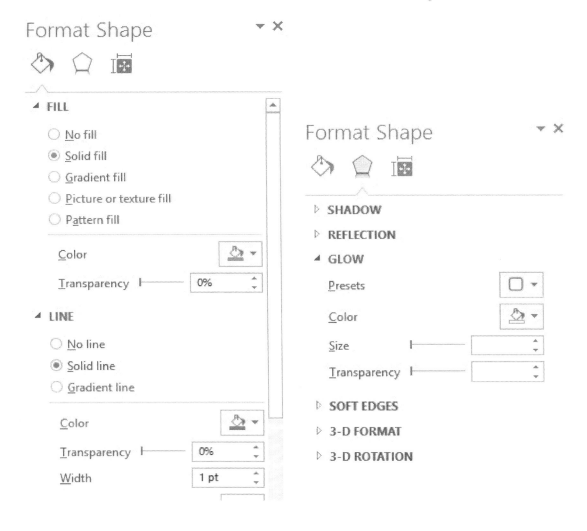

More on Outlook Email Messaging

To start creating a new item on Outlook (mail, contact, task, appointment ...etc), you may click New Items and choose the item to create from the drop down menu:

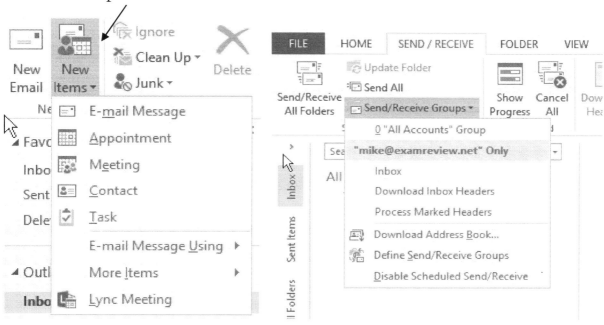

You want to know that new emails you create will first sit and wait in the Outbox. The SEND/RECEIVE ribbon allows you to initiate the sending and receiving of emails. Send/Receive Groups allows you to choose the account to send and receive. Emails successfully sent will go into the Sent Items folder. If a message gets stuck in the Outbox, something is wrong. Permissions is an option that requires server side work – there has to be a digital rights management server in place. Requesting receipt, however, can usually work without a digital rights management server. You do want to know the difference between a delivery receipt and a read receipt. The former confirms delivery of the email message you sent, while the latter also confirms that your message was opened.

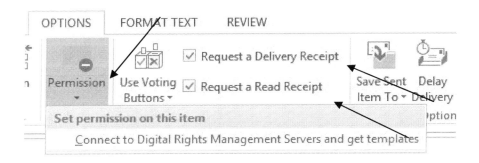

You can click Tracking and set more options.

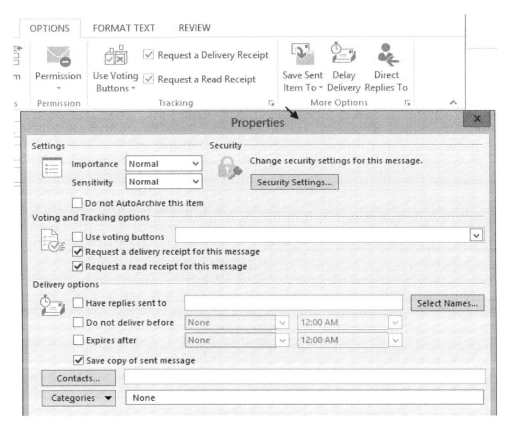

You can create a poll in the message via voting buttons. The available buttons are Approve;Reject, Yes;No, Yes;No;Maybe, and Custom. However, the recipients must also be using Outlook in order for this to work.

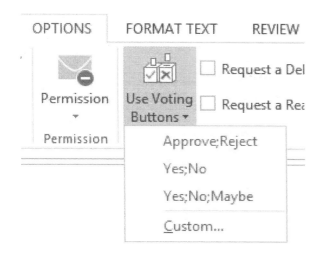

To make it easy to send emails to a team, you can use the Team Email feature. There is a first time setup procedure to go through and once that is done you can send emails to the entire team without the need to specify the individual team recipients.

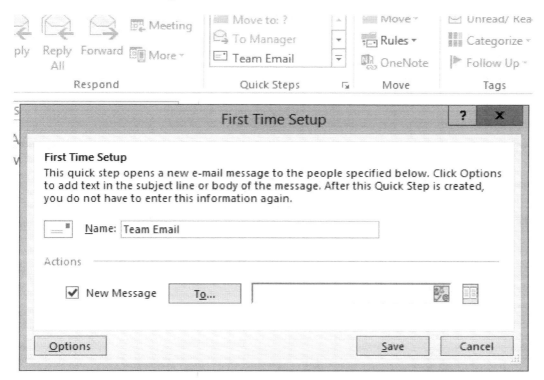

HOME – Junk provides options for dealing with junk emails. You want to know that the Outlook Junk Email Filter cannot stop delivery of junk emails. However, you can use it to move those emails to the Junk Email folder. By default, Outlook has the Junk Email Filter turned on with a protection level of No Automatic Filtering. You can change the level to something more aggressive, just that there is never any absolute guarantee on the accuracy.

For further in-depth configuration you should choose Junk E-mail Options…

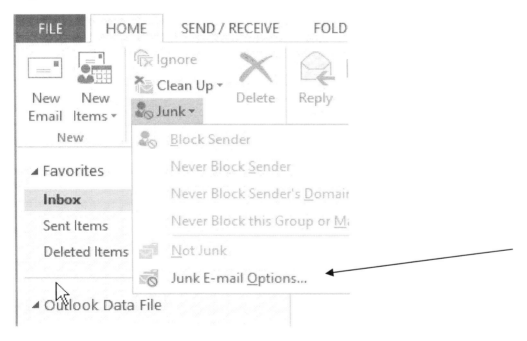

The options available here are pretty self explanatory:

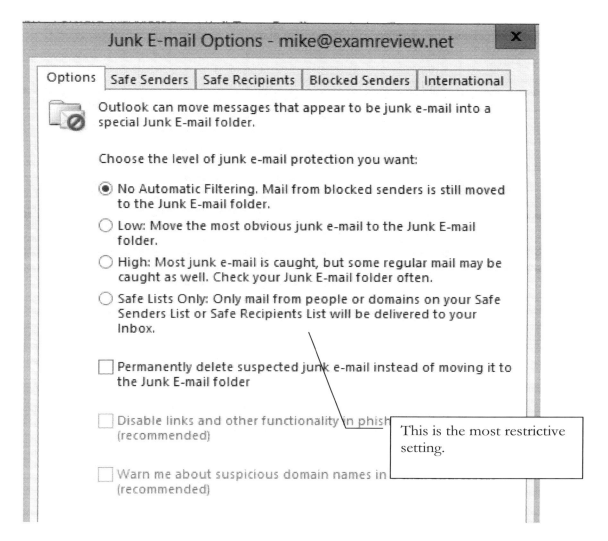

To make sure the innocent senders you know will never encounter troubles when sending you emails, you want to add them to the Safe Senders List. Email addresses and domain names listed as Safe Senders will never be treated as junk email. On the other hand, you may block messages from certain bad senders by having their email addresses or domain names added to the Blocked Senders List so that whatever they send you will always be moved to the Junk Email folder.

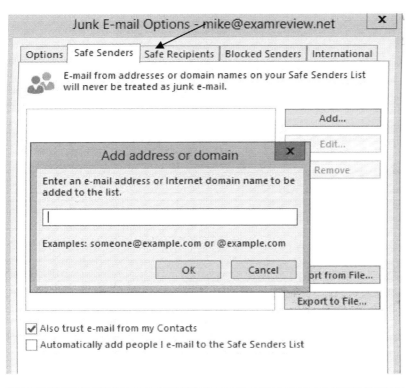
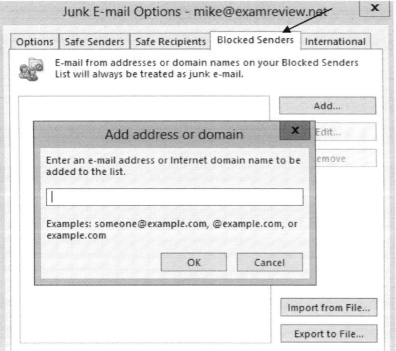

International - Blocked Top-Level Domains List is primarily for blocking all unwanted email messages from a certain country or region.

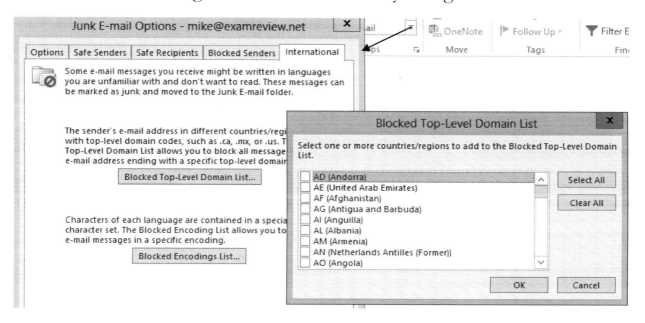

VIEW – Change View allows you to only change the way email messages are displayed on screen. Simply put, changing view has no impact on the actual message contents.

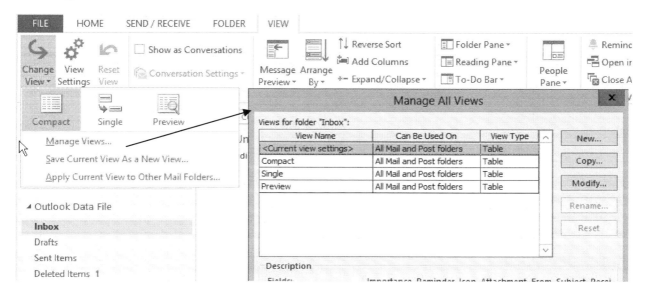

Do note that if you go to VIEW – Message Preview you can specify the number of lines of each piece of email that can be previewed through the folder listing pane. The default is one line. If your screen is small you can turn this preview off entirely. On the other hand, if you have plenty of space you can set it to 3 lines max.

FOLDER – AutoArchive Settings allows you to configure automatic archiving.

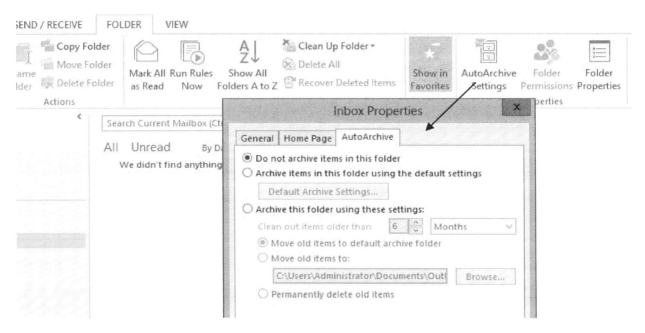

The default setting is to run autoarchive every 14 days. You can specify what Outlook should do during the autoarchive process, as seen on the coming screenshot (all the available options are self explanatory):

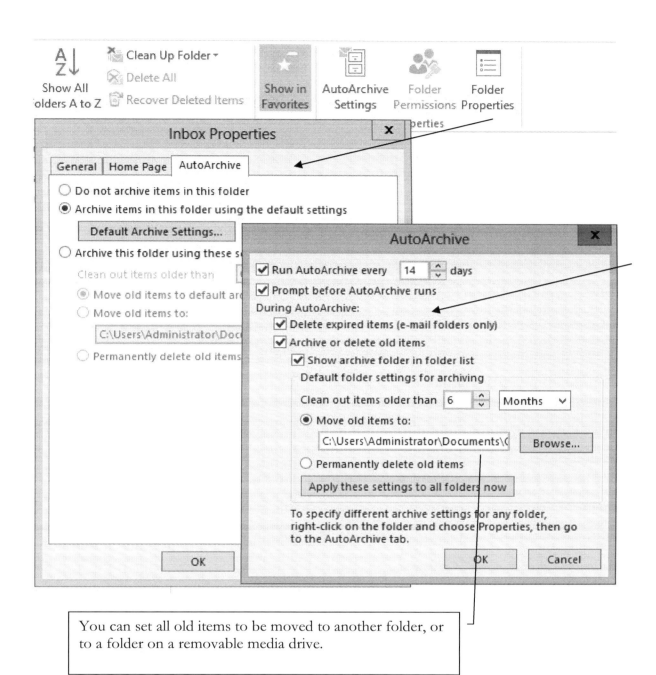

You can set all old items to be moved to another folder, or to a folder on a removable media drive.

Outlook Scheduling

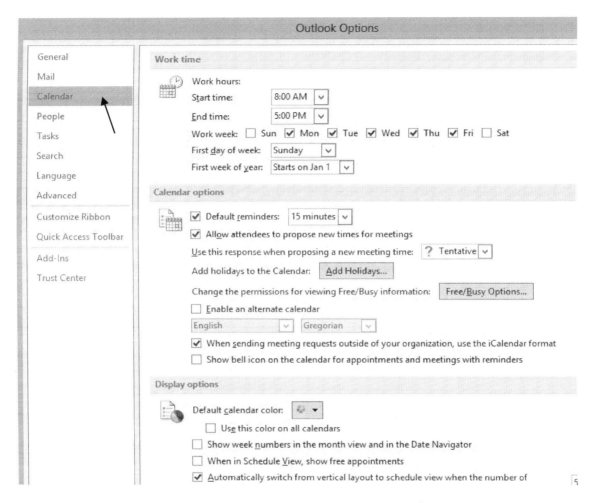

Calendar serves as both a calendar and a meeting / appointment scheduler. A meeting is in fact an appointment to which you ask people to join (through email) and request resources to be reserved. You can send meeting requests and reserve resources for actual in person meetings or virtual online meetings. All communications take place through Outlook messaging (in other words, email is the "backbone" of the system). Before using the calendar functions you want to first go to FILE and then configure the Calendar options, such as your office hours, the reminder intervals ...etc. You want these to exactly match your official office protocols. And if you want people to know your schedule, you should configure the Internet Free/Busy Options. The Publish at location option should be provided by your network administrator since it is a feature that requires server side coordination.

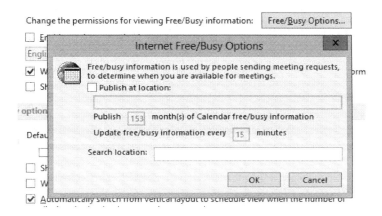

Unlike Outlook Options, settings available in Calendar Properties are on a per calendar basis. AutoArchive can be configured on a per calendar basis here. By default cleanup is done automatically every 6 months.

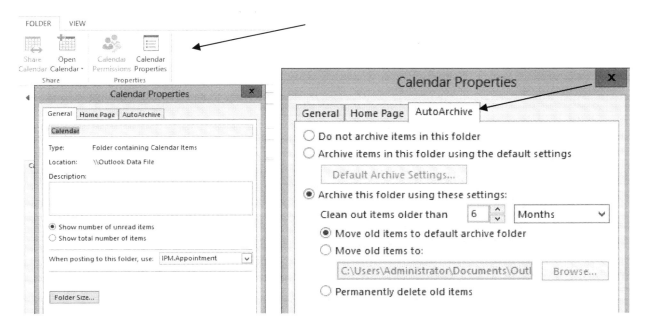

If your company network has Exchange Server, you can share your calendar with other peoples who also have Exchange accounts (they need to be granted permissions to view yours). You do this via HOME - Share - Share Calendar. The relevant menu options are available only if you have logged in via an Exchange account. Or, you can simply share the calendar via email by right clicking on a calendar and choose Share – Email Calendar.

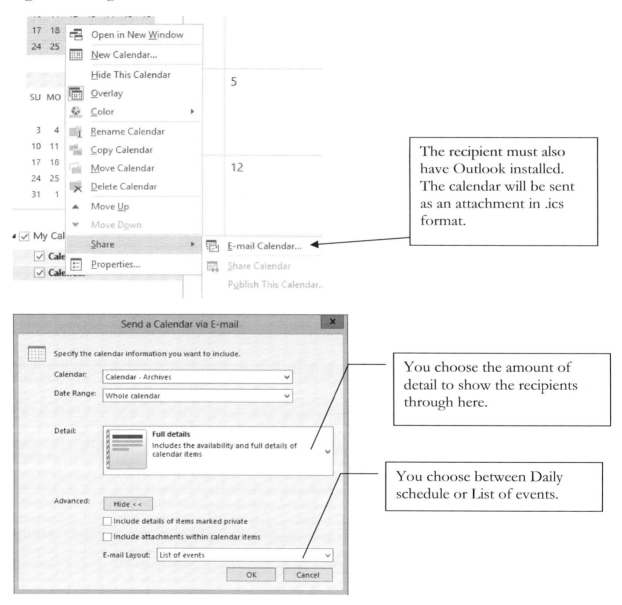

You can display your calendar on a Day, Work Week, Week or Month basis. You can also change your Calendar View by clicking Change View. You can even customize the formatting and choose Save Current View as New View.

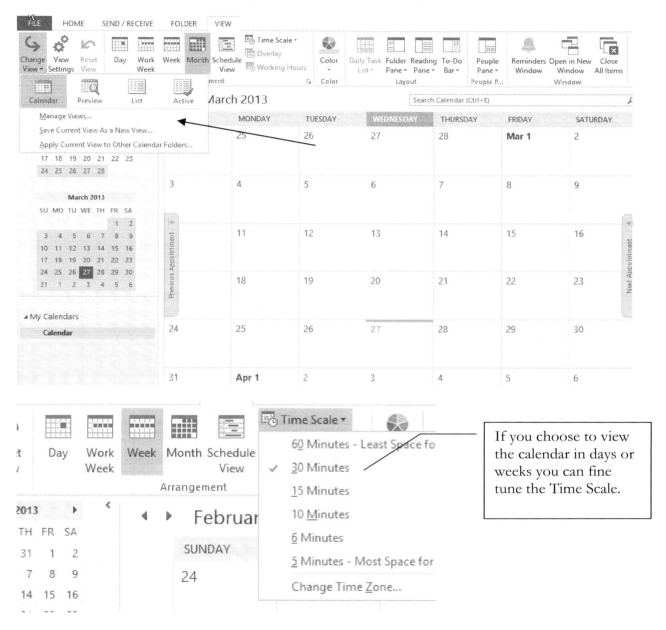

You can also view more than one calendar at the same time side-by-side or as an overlaid stack. You do this via the Navigation pane on the left hand side. This pane is available if you click All Folders on the left.

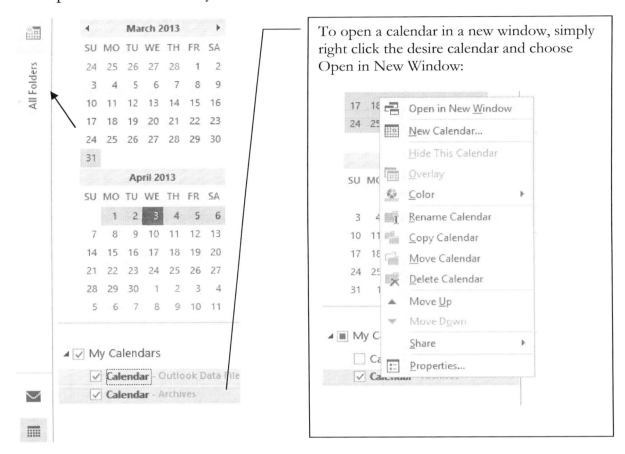

If you click multiple calendars you can view them side by side. To view in overlay mode, choose VIEW – Overlay.

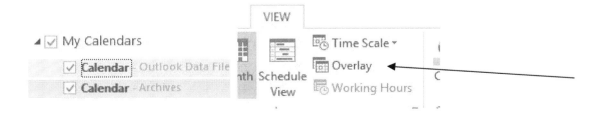

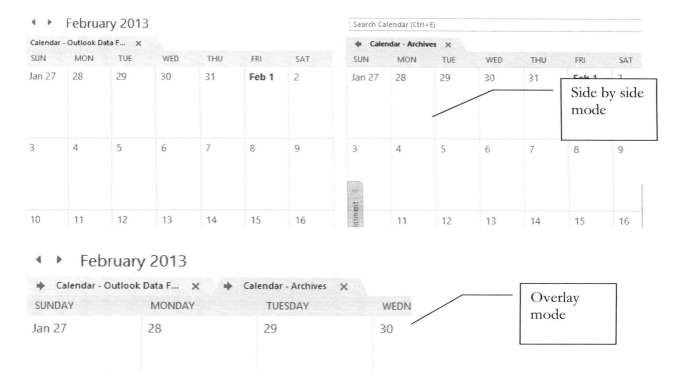

Appointment and Scheduling are available via the APPOINTMENT ribbon. To create new appointment, event or meeting request, a shortcut way is to right click on a date and choose what to create:

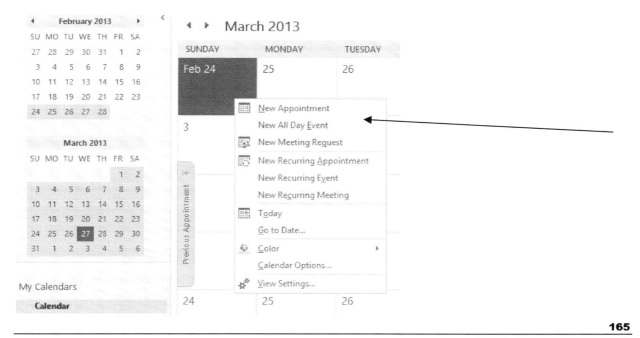

An appointment involves yourself only. You can use an appointment to block out time in your calendar. The most straight forward way to set up one is to type directly on a calendar date:

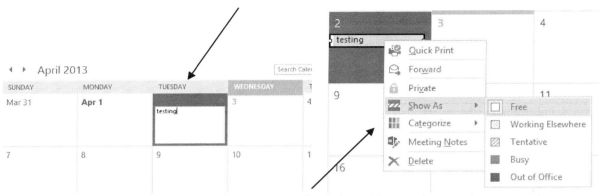

To block out time, right click on it and pick a Show As option, or choose Delete to remove it. To move the appointment, just drag it around.

A more detailed way is to click New Appointment. You go to the Subject box to type a description. You then go to the Location box and type the location. You can enter the start and end times, OR type in any specific words or phrases instead of regular dates. You may also show to others whether you are available by going to Options and then choose Free, Working Elsewhere, Tentative, Busy or Out of Office.

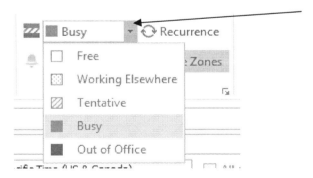

To turn this appointment into a recurring one, in Options you click Recurrence and then choose a pattern of Daily, Weekly, Monthly, or Yearly. The default is once a week.

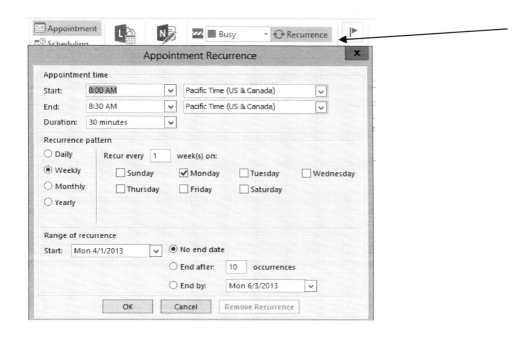

You can click on Time Zones and then pick the time zone for the start time and the end time. You can use different time zones on them.

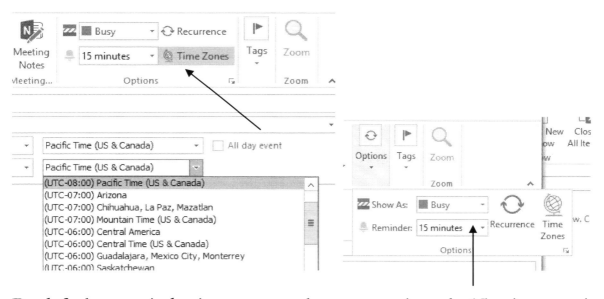

By default a reminder is set up to show approximately 15 minutes prior to the appointment. You can click on the little bell like icon and pick a time, or click Sound… to choose another reminder sound effect.

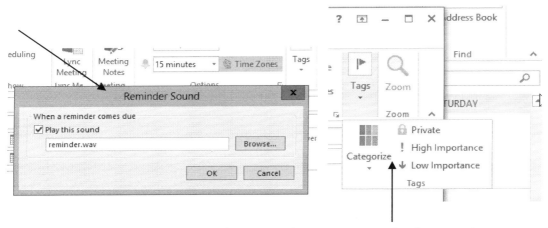

You can optionally have the appointment marked as private so that other people cannot see its details. You do so via Tags - Private. Still, the most secure way to stop other people from reading it would be to NOT grant them read permission to your calendar.

An all day event refers to an activity that lasts for the whole day but it does not block out any time in your calendar day. Some examples of such event are anniversary, birthday, holiday...etc. A meeting blocks out time and also involves other Outlook users (you invite them to attend).

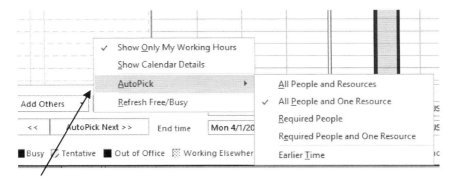

Autopick is a feature that works with Exchange Server to find the next available free period for your meeting attendees. After you add attendees to the meeting request, Outlook will look for and read the attendees' free/busy status and then come up with the best possible times that are available on the selected date. It will also list the time and number of attendees who will be available.

You need to realize that it is the current time zone setting on your local computer that is used for scheduling meetings. If necessary you can always go to Options and change the time zone to something else.

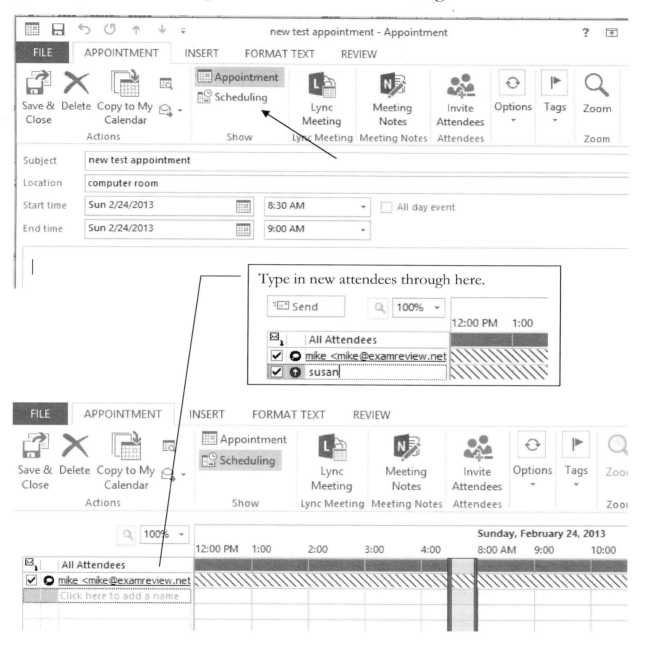

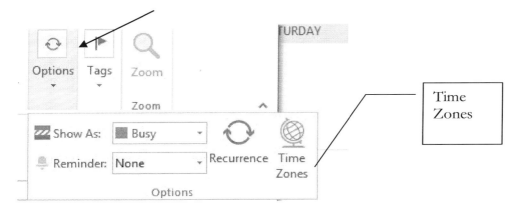

You can forward appointments as emails to someone else. You choose Forward to forward to another Outlook user. You forward via the iCalendar format for those who use other email readers.

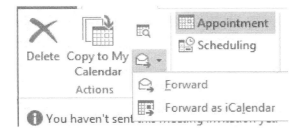

You can also copy meetings from someone else's calendar to yours. However, to keep receiving updates you must choose between the options shown below:

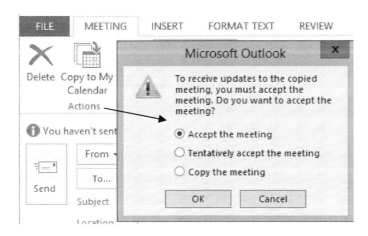

If you want to take notes for the meeting, click on Meeting Notes and choose Take notes on your own. Under AutoPreview, you can simply hover with your mouse on the corresponding appointment to see the notes.

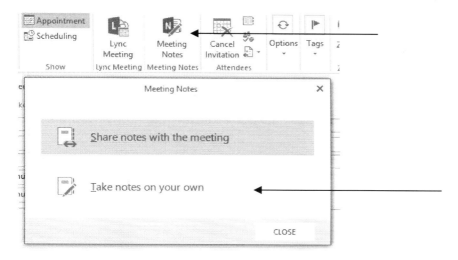

If you need to translate certain text into a different language, highlight the desired text and choose REVIEW - Translate – Translate selected text.

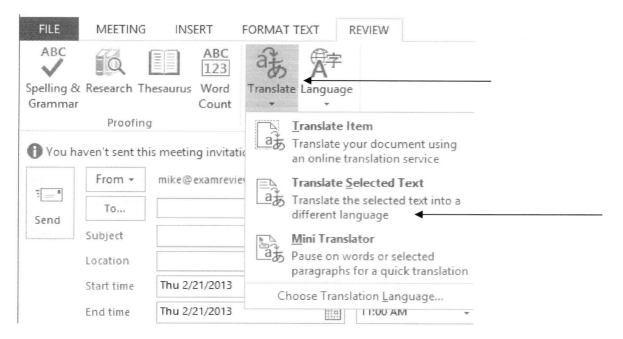

Tasks and Notes

You use a task to track a work all the way until completion. A to-do item is simply an Outlook item flagged for follow-up. A task flagged for follow-up (the default setting makes a new task flagged automatically) is a to-do item.

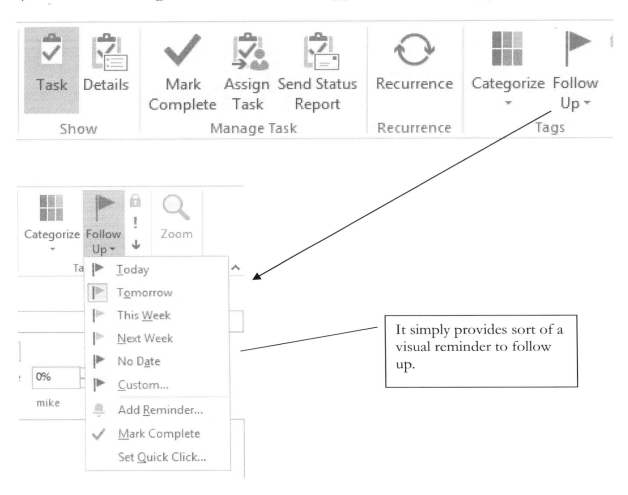

It simply provides sort of a visual reminder to follow up.

You click HOME – New Items – Task to create a new task. You then specify the subject, dates, reminder, status and priority accordingly. The possible statuses are Not Started (0% completed), In Progress, Waiting on someone else, Deferred or Completed (100%).

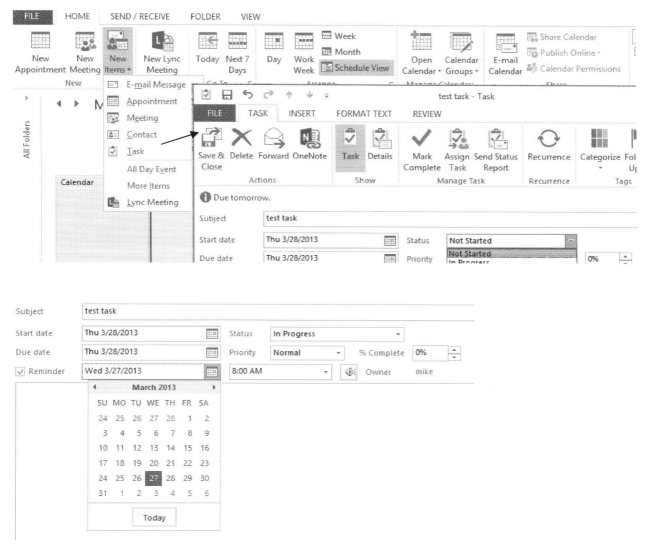

You can click Assign Task to assign a task to another Outlook user. Assigning a task means sending a task request to someone. The person who receives your request can decline or accept the task or assign the task to someone else. Whoever accepts the task becomes the task owner, which is the only entity who can make changes to the task, although all copies of the changed task will be updated as well. The whole task assignment process requires server side coordination by the Exchange Server.

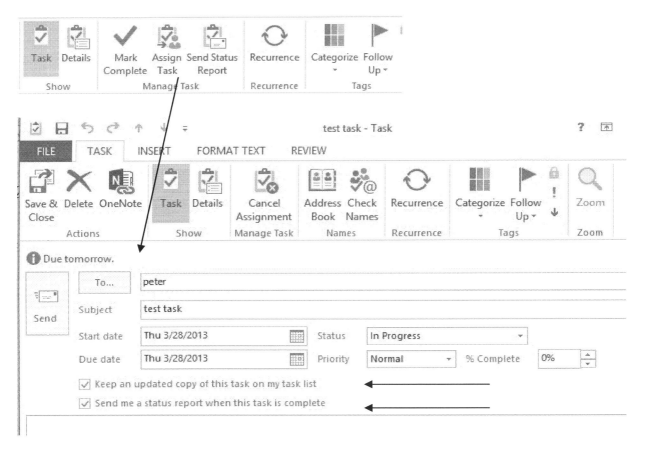

Technically you can assign a task to more than one person. However, by doing this you will not be able to keep an updated copy. You should therefore assign each task to one person only whenever possible. Tasks assigned will show in your task list. And you can use these two very useful features to make tracking easy (they are checked by default): Keep an updated copy of this task on my task list and Send me a status report when this task is complete.

You can reclaim a rejected task assignment by opening the declined task message (when an assignment is rejected you will be messaged) and choosing Return to Task List. Forwarding a task simply means forwarding it to another person to track. It is NOT the same as assigning a task. To send a status report of a task as email, click Send Status Report.

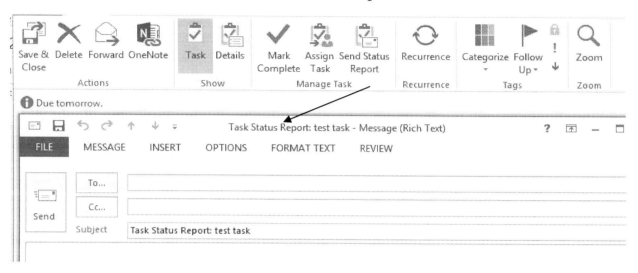

Notes are simply visual notes you use to give yourself a reminder on something. You can add notes in any folder. The shortcut key combination to add one is Ctrl Shift N.

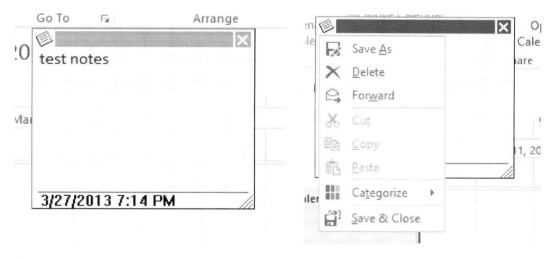

After creating one you simply click on the upper left icon and choose the desired option.

Contacts and Contact Groups

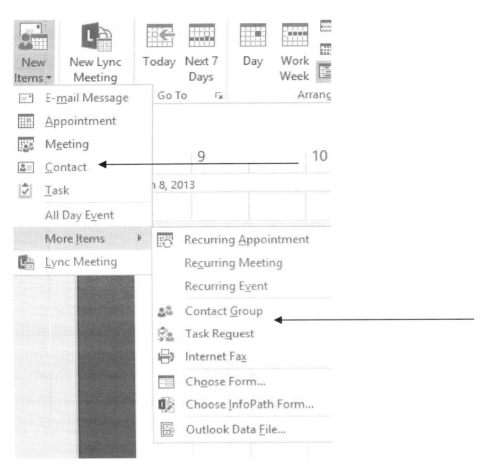

The Outlook Address Book OAB stores all address books and address lists created from the various contact folders. By default these contact folders are automatically created in the Outlook Address Book. You can use different folders to store different kinds of contacts (it is all about organizing your contacts).

You create a new contact by clicking New Items – Contact. You use a contact group to group commonly used contacts (it is about further organizing contacts within a folder). You click New Items – More Items – Contact Group to create one. The available options are pretty much self-explanatory.

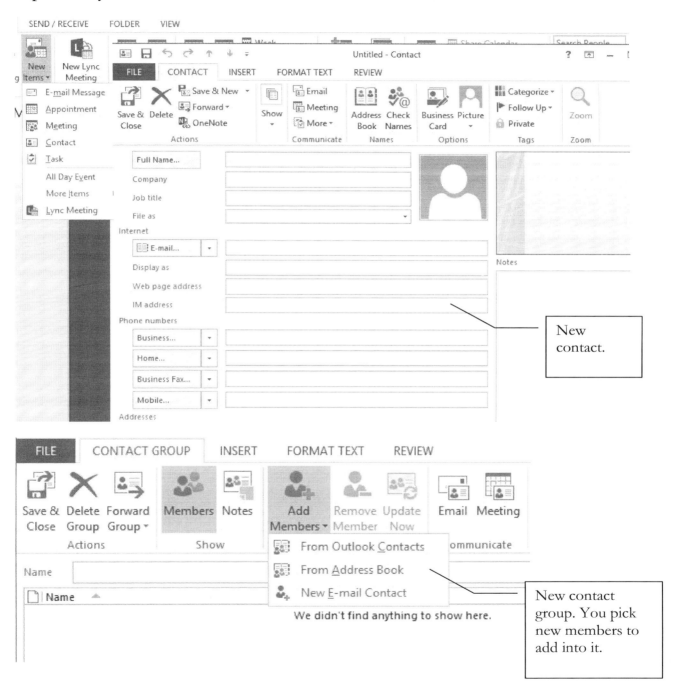

To add a note for the group, simply click Notes.

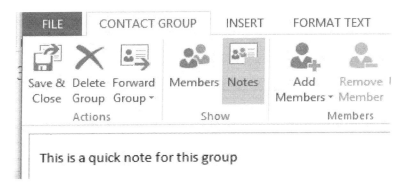

You want to know that flags can actually be applied to contacts to give a visible reminder for taking an action related to this contact. The task view will show the flagged contacts.

Also note that a contact group is not the same as a distribution list. A distribution list is simply a group of email addresses added to the Outlook Address Book as a single address. You use such a list to send emails to multiple recipients conveniently. it is not for organizing contacts.

End of book

Made in the USA
Lexington, KY
27 June 2013